Hellinger

The Churches and their God

Hellinger Publications

Published by
Hellinger Publications
Sonnleitstraße 37
83404 Bischofswiesen
Germany
Postfach 2120
83462 Berchtesgaden
www.Hellinger.com

Cover:
Manuela Erdödy

Design:
Büro A34, Helmut Gebhardt
www.a34-vis.com

Translated by Angelika Schenk
Revised and edited by Suzi
Tucker

ISBN 978-3-942808-23-1

11 10 9 8 7 6 5 4 3 2 **1**
2016 2015 2014 **2013**

Hellinger

The Churches and their God

Hellinger Publications

Introduction

I have been well acquainted with the church for a long time. After all, as a priest and monk I was intensely involved in the life of the church over many years. As a missionary with the Zulus in South Africa I was at the forefront of the endeavor to spread the message of the church and to gain new believers.

On the personal side I am essentially indebted to the church. The church was my home for a long period. It was the decisive family in which I was able to develop in many ways. Therefore I felt close and connected to it in a deep way, similar to how a child feels towards his mother.

I studied theology and I became well versed in the doctrines and the history of the church, and as a member of a spiritual order I also grew deeply acquainted with its piety and devotion.

In recent years I have had the opportunity to look at many issues far more closely, and through my intense consideration of Jesus and in my studies of the Bible I became aware of many contradictions. Beyond that, I could see the secret sources from the time before the New Testament that put the Church and Jesus into a perspective that demanded clarification, and I came to question much about the image of Jesus as it was recorded, and also about the image of the church. The same is true for many of its rituals.

Above all, my work led me to become occupied extensively with the suffering of people and their backgrounds. I could see some of the hidden sources from which many ailments were fed. I could see which paths led human beings out of their entanglements with the backgrounds of suffering, and into another freedom. These paths demanded the farewell from the church and the farewell from both its promises and its threats.

In this book I am moving into these insights and into a consciousness that opens our eyes and leads us on the path to an all-embracing freedom. In this I feel especially close to the first victim of binding doctrines and images, and over large distances, I move on by his side. The first victim of the church was its so-called founder, Jesus.

Was anyone in the church's history motivated by bad intentions? Am I allowed to reproach anyone? Am I allowed to reproach myself?

In all of this, other creative powers were and are at work. Therefore, in what I query in this book, I follow my trails in accord with a love that includes us all. I submit to it. So much is at stake.

This book is not an attempt on my part to initiate a movement of reformation within the church. Nothing essential in it can be reformed, for even the slightest attempt to wish for this or act in this direction endangers the church as a whole. This is a matter of all or nothing.

In this sense I am not available for any discussions and debates about what is said here. Having said what was important for me, I withdraw. How? With love for the churches as well.

Hellinger

Jesus

The Church

Other mythological backgrounds

Emptiness

The earth

Applied freedom

Ecumenicalism

Appendix

Jesus

Jesus

From afar, hardly recognizable any more, through the many who usurped you, I salute you: remembering and also forgetting you at the same time.

Son of man, one of us, who, failing, experienced the ultimate, and in the face of the ultimate taught us to be humble, powerless, and exactly like this to be in complete surrender. You have done away with the distinction of good and bad before God. And still, you were banished to the faraway heavens and proclaimed the judge over good and bad, by those who would not bear your greatness, so as to avenge your death on those whom you invited to your table. What have they done to you through this!

Instead of being allowed to love on this earth as you did, without excluding even the least person, we must now fear you as if you had not also loved the least ones before God, like all the others.

Therefore I will forget how you are being disfigured and wielded as a sword in the hands of others, and I will remember how you pronounced all as equally worthy of god's love.

Thus I take you into my soul and I beg of you that you teach me in my soul.

Good Friday

On Good Friday Christians remember the crucifixion of Jesus, his terrible death stretched out between heaven and earth. He died between two offenders who shared the same death with him.

Was the God of Jesus closer to any one of them? Was He both close to and distant from all three of them equally? Was this a bloody spectacle being performed between heaven and earth? Or just on the level of earth, and only amongst people who referred to the same god, that god who was meant to testify through this crucifixion that he was on their side? Or perhaps on the other side? All in his name?

These executions continued after the death of these crucified men, still in the name of the same god, to this very day. Did they also continue on the eve of this Good Friday, when the pope bound the Catholic priests to celibacy with sharp words, still crucifying them that way? Are the Christians not still called to bear their cross, together with Jesus?

Nowadays however, to Jesus' followers, Good Friday seems to be just a preliminary step to his resurrection on the third day.

The question comes up: Did Jesus really rise from the dead? The reports in the gospels appear contradictory, as if added later to take the sting out of the crucifixion and the Good Friday. Those still following Jesus along the stations of the cross are supposed to be encouraged to carry their cross in the hope that they may also rise from the dead with him.

About which god is all of this ultimately? What happens to the risen Jesus, now called the Christ, when he comes again, as Christians hope? Or do they have to fear his second coming? Perhaps he will come back as the judge over life and death, according to what the bible says?

What happens to those he rejects? Are they bound for eternal damnation? Who can be certain of being counted amongst the chosen ones who may enter his eternal Kingdom?

Good Friday makes them hopeful, provided they follow Jesus on his path to his crucifixion until the end of life.

Have I gone too far here? Or do we gain hope if we take Good Friday seriously, grieving Jesus' death with him on this day, his death without resurrection? Do we really only then look into the countenance of the god of Jesus? Into his bloody countenance? Do we also look into the faces of those who admonish us in the name of the crucified Jesus to carry the cross with him? What an inhuman face! What an ungodly face!

So how do we look at the crucified Jesus on Good Friday? We look at him in horror. This is supposed to be God's son? Abandoned by his God in such a terrible way? Executed like that by God in his name?

I look at him as one of us, as one forsaken by this god, by this god according to our image.

How can I live after that? I can live differently, because I know my life in other hands, in the hands of life, as it was given to me, together with all others and everything else that lives, by a creative power. By a power to which I find my way without carrying a cross, lovingly at one with everything alive?

Risen from the dead

In the apostolic credo the Christians profess of Jesus of Nazareth:

Risen from the dead,
he ascended into heaven,
and is seated at the right hand of the Father,
from where he will come again in glory
to judge the living and the dead, and his
kingdom will have no end.

Which image is behind this idea, given that the Christians expect that they will also rise from the dead in their physical body when Jesus returns on the day of judgment? They expect to physically ascend to heaven and sit with Jesus at the right hand of God.

At the same time it says in the bible that upon his return the risen Jesus will say to those he rejected: "Get away from me, you cursed ones, into the eternal fire that is prepared for the devil and his angels." Here we also find the idea that the rejected are physically thrown into this fire, for they are also resurrected in their physical body.

Did Jesus really say this? Obviously this sentence was put into his mouth by others, for it contradicts everything that Jesus said in the Sermon On the Mount about his father in heaven. He called him merciful, for he lets the sun rise over the good and the bad, and he lets it rain over the just and the unjust. Jesus himself showed merciful conduct in the same way. Therefore he was judged to be a friend of sinners, by some who deemed themselves to be just. When other just people demanded of Jesus that he condemn an adulteress to death through stoning, in accord with the laws of Moses, Jesus replied: "He amongst you who is free from sin, throw the first stone."

Would he say the same on the day of judgment to those who expect him to throw the so-called sinners into hell for eternity? He himself prayed during his crucifixion for those who nailed him to the cross: "Father forgive them for they know not what they are doing." Can this prayer be reconciled with the passage in the bible about the day of judgment? It forces us to be merciful like him and to forgive ourselves and others from the heart whatever they do to us and others, and whatever we to ourselves and them.

Which resurrection?

A further question: If Jesus rose from the dead physically, and went to heaven physically, what kind of god is expecting him? Is this god also in a physical body? If he weren't, how should Jesus sit on his right side, and from there return and make all people rise from the dead physically? And then he calls some into heaven physically, and throws the others into hell physically?

What kind of an image of God and of heaven is at work here? Is God not described like a worldly ruler with His court above which He reigns?

Again, the question: Where are the dead now? Are the good in heaven, and how are they in heaven? With which god are they? Are they with a god who has no body, a god who eschews them physically?

Further, are the deceased already in heaven after a judicial verdict? Have they already been condemned to hell, and into what kind of a hell, and by whom?

We can see there's no end to questions and contradictions.

The former and the later lives

I will also speak about the physical resurrection from yet another perspective and point out the contradictions that make it look rather unlikely. I will stay close to what remains within our experience.

The experience of former and later lives is spread over the whole world, meaning that we are born more than once and also die more than once, having a different body each time. Yet via the soul, our next body takes on parts of the genetics of our former bodies, which come back to life and live on in a clearly defined way.

Where do we dwell in the time in between, without a body? In which way do we continue with our existence in the interim?

Obviously we live on with a sense of self even without a body, yet still with feelings and with knowledge that reaches beyond our current knowledge. We experience the non-physical presence of the dead, for instance, when they haunt us. A clear example is when people die in a accident, and then subsequent accidents happen in the same location and other people die in similar ways. Apparently they are drawn into death by those who died there before and still inhabit this place. In England the term "black spot" refers to this phenomenon.

On the other hand we are also visited by dead people in a friendly and caring way. They are also without a body, and yet are alive and present. Thus a dead mother visits her child sometimes in a helping way. Some healers are visibly sought out and taken possession of by a power, so that this power achieves healing through them. During this time the healers appear possessed by the soul of some dead person whose name they might even know. The healers then speak and move like these people, until their healing task is completed, and they return to their normal selves, without knowing what happened through them.

Obviously many dead dwell in an interim space. For how long, and to which purpose, remains hidden from us. They are all without their body, which lies in the grave, and which has long been stripped of what returns to earth.

Perhaps these dead are waiting for a new life in a new body, hoping to experience something in a new body that is waiting for them.

The belief in physical resurrection

In the light of these experiences and observations, the idea of physical resurrection of our present bodies and the physical resurrection of Jesus and his physical return on judgment day, together with the physical resurrection of all the dead, appears to be fraught with contradictions.

Yet the Christian belief with its expectations and with its demands on its believers, designed to avoid the last judgment, is based on this belief, including the inherent contradictions.

The question is: When we release ourselves from this belief in a physical resurrection and a final judgment day, where do we experience ourselves led in this life?

We feel ourselves exceptionally guided, with a beginning before which there was already a lot, and with an end that will continue on several times in this world, and with an interim time and with several interim times that may last a long time for many.

In the interim time we perhaps conduct ourselves well, kindly disposed towards the living and helpful to others. Perhaps we are supporting them in a knowing way, and making their life rich and great, staying by their side like guardian angels.

Or perhaps we behave in the opposite way in this interim time, like beings that envy the living.

Perhaps we might have to possess some of the living in a way that enables them to achieve something, that even forces them to set something in motion that ultimately costs many lives and takes many years afterwards to rebuild and to bring back into order what was destroyed.

Of course we go through the same as the living. We are haunted by our past lives, but also haunted by the former lives of others, taken into possession, to heal or to destroy. We submit to a movement that appears given to us and yet leaves some room for us in which we can personally further and complete something.

Much remains to be said. But in spite of that I will tell you a story now, a story of peace.

The turning point

A boy is born into his family, his homeland and his culture, and even as a child he hears who was their hero, their teacher and their master, and he feels the deepest longing to become like him, to be like him.

He joins up with like-minded people, practices hard discipline for years, and follows the great example, until he has become like him, until he thinks, speaks, feels and wills like him.

Still he believes that something is missing. So he sets out on a long journey to the furthest isolated point in order to perhaps cross one last frontier. He passes by old gardens that were abandoned long ago. Wild roses are still flowering, and tall trees bear their autumn fruit that's falling to the ground uncared for; there is no one to collect it. From here on it is desert country.

And soon an unknown emptiness surrounds him. It is as if all the directions are the same, and what appears before him, he soon recognizes as empty too. He wanders on in aimlessness; he loses the connection to his senses. And then he finds himself before a spring. It comes up from the earth and quickly seeps back into the sand again. And where the water goes, the desert is transformed into a paradise.

As he looks around, he sees two strangers coming. They had done exactly as he had done, following their hero, until they were like him. They, too, had set out on an arduous journey into the desert's loneliness to meet the last frontier. And like him, they found the spring. Together, they bend down to drink from the same water, and they believe themselves to be quite near their destination. They tell each other what their names are: "My name is Gautama, the Buddha." "My name is Jesus, the Christ." "My name is Mohammed, the Prophet."

But then the night falls and surrounds them as though for eons, with the far-off splendor of the silent stars. No words, no sounds, and one of the three knows he is close to his beloved master like he never was before. It is as if for just a moment, he could get a glimpse of how it was for him when he did know: so powerless, so futile, and so small. And how it would be if he knew about the guilt as well. He then heard him inwardly say: If they left me with the dead, I would find my peace.

The next morning the young man turns back and he escapes the desert. His path leads once more past the lonely gardens, and takes him further to the garden that's his own. Before the gate an old man greets him. He says: "He who finds his way back from so far away must love the fertile earth. He knows that everything that grows will also die, and when its life ends, it will nourish others." "Yes," says the returning one, "I agree, these are the laws on this dear earth." And thus he begins to cultivate it.

The Church

The beginnings of the Church

The Church professes its belief in Jesus of Nazareth as its founder. It gathers those around it who refer to Jesus as their redeemer. Referring to the risen Jesus, who through his resurrection revealed himself as god's anointed one, as Christos in Greek, these believers call themselves Christians.

However, this Church was only established after Jesus' death. In this Church the scattered disciples gathered after his crucifixion. Through the belief in his resurrection they joined as an ad hoc community awaiting his return.

Who may belong to the Church?

In the beginning the Church was only for Jews. They saw in Jesus the Messiah whom they were waiting for. Therefore they believed that only Jews were allowed to belong to their community, including others who converted to Judaism.

The opening of the originally Jewish Church to the heathens also was only decided at the first apostolic council in Jerusalem, in the year 49/50, under the considerable influence of Paul, who saw himself as an apostle of the heathens. He, together with other apostles, including Peter, convinced the participants that the church had to open up to the heathens, and that Jesus was their messiah too. From thereon the originally Jewish Church turned into a universal Church, embracing all.

The new Christians were introduced to this extended Church through baptism. This inclusion created and cemented a new division, the separation between the baptized and the non-baptized. Just as earlier when the heathens were excluded from the Jewish church and only included through baptism, from now on the non-baptized were to be excluded. This division still asserts itself.

How was this division and exclusion explained then, and how is it justified even today? With a doctrine for which there is no reasonable and biblically tenable justification. It is the doctrine of the original sin. It states that a child does not only receive life from the parents, but that he or she remains expelled from paradise, like the parents, together with the ancient ancestors Adam and Eve. Only baptism can restore the access to paradise and to the tree of life. How drastically this doctrine has been applied one can see in the practice of preventing children who died soon after birth before they were baptised from being buried within the cemetery reserved for Christians only.

This practice is in opposition to what the bible reports Jesus thinking and wanting, as found in Luke 18: 15 – 16.

"People also brought children to him so that he touched them. When the disciples saw that, they wanted to scold the parents; but Jesus called them over and said: Let the children come to me and don't stop them! For theirs is the kingdom of God. Truly I say to you, who does not take the kingdom of God like a child, will surely not enter it."

Here we need to acknowledge that Jesus never said anything about an original sin, and there is no verse in the bible about the need of some baptism through which this original sin is repaid and the separation from God done away with again. On the contrary. Jesus said something about God that does away with all such ideas. It is in the Sermon On the Mountain in Matthew.

"Love your enemies and pray for those who persecute you, so that you become children of your father in heaven. He lets the sun rise over good and bad and he lets the rain fall over the just and the unjust."

Just as the Church opposed this teaching and this way of conduct, it took the same approach in other spheres of life. I will mention two here, two essential ones, though: marriage, and sexual longing and expression.

Marriage

Marriage existed long before the institution of the Church, as the enduring union of man and woman. It had the aim of procreation and of providing long-term protection and care that would enable the children to eventually also enter into a committed union with a partner, to become a couple and also father and mother.

The forms of this partnership vary, including polygamy, which granted women and children comprehensive security, even beyond the death of a woman. In its care for the children, polygamy goes beyond monogamy in many ways, as I observed it among the Zulus in South Africa. For instance, if a woman's husband died, the man's brother would take in the woman and the children, alongside his wife and children. There was no abandonment or additional suffering for the wife or for the children.

The Church intervened in this form of marriage, declaring that marriage is a sacrament dictating monogamy. With this intervention, the Church took the place of many different orders in different societies. For instance, it created a law about the insolubility of marriage and the prohibition of premarital and extramarital sexual relationships. These were declared deadly sins by the Church. In this, the sixth of the Ten Commandments that originally only prohibited adultery was extended to any non- marital sexual relationship, including a new marriage after divorce, and even to any personal sexual satisfaction. As a consequence divorced partners in a new marriage were excluded from the sacraments, as if they were engaged in constant sin. In this way sexual purity was raised to an ideal that ignores that behind the sexual desire a creative power is at work, a power serving life in the most comprehensive way. In the depth and consequences of the sexual drive, there is no comparison to any other human function.

Who is allowed to interfere with this human desire and this deep satisfaction with damnation and restriction? Who is allowed to intervene through restricting laws, punishing so-called transgressions of these laws with exclusion from the church and thereby exposing people to damnation?

Jesus also spoke of the irreversibility of marriage, yet without condemning adultery. Completing the story mentioned earlier, when Pharisees and scribes wanted to convince Jesus to agree to stoning an adulteress, according to Mosaic law, Jesus said: 'Who amongst you who is without sin, throw the first stone." Then he bent down to give everyone the opportunity to leave. After a while they had all disappeared. Jesus straightened up and asked the woman: "Where are they? Did no one condemn you?"

She replied: "None, master."

And Jesus said to her: "I do not condemn you either."

The sexual desire

The sexual desire, as irresistible as we may experience it, follows an inner order. Above all, it binds the partners in a lasting way. After sexual union nothing remains as before. Therefore the uninhibited does not only bring gain, it comes at a price.

Is there a rule to this? Can the height exclude the depth or vice versa? Only where the river can flow from the source to its destination can it gather all of its confluents and thus, together with them, reach the shared destination.

Of course there are orders to protect the family. Nowadays they are enforced by governmental institutions, independent of the churches, for the welfare of many.

What would be the solution here?

The church hands the solution back to the worldly order. Here, too, like God, it lets its sun shine over the good and the bad, and it lets the rain fall over the just and the unjust, with love.

The edifice of doctrine

I nearly wrote "the deficit of doctrine." But I will stick to the heading. However, I will shed some light on the structural condition of this edifice.

The Church is held together through a firm edifice of doctrine. This means it is held together through defined sentences that everyone who wishes to belong must agree to. This means the members of the Church must believe these sentences and confess to them in the Credo by reciting it publicly together with the other believers, for instance in Mass.

Apart from this credo, which sums up a selection of doctrines, there are others that are explained and passed on to the students of theology and above all to the future priests, in the so-called dogmatics. In this sense I became acquainted with these dogmatics over a number of years.

The movements towards reform

In the church there are movements of reforming again and again. The last great one of them we experienced following the second Vatican council under Popes John the 23rd and Paul the sixth.

The impetus of this reform movement petered out so that presently we experience a restoration movement. No wonder! These reform movements repeatedly fail in the face of the same question. This question was excluded in all these movements of reform; therefore, I will address it here in a direct and open way.

These doctrines state something that cannot be verified, not even as they are imparted to the believers as true, for they are always caught up in contradictions.

Jesus the son of God

The first dogma is that Jesus is the one sent to us by God to announce God's truth to us. This refers to the New Testament in which Jesus' utterances are recorded and declared to be a revelation of God that each believer must agree to.

We need to keep in mind here that in the first three centuries after Jesus' death many of his followers saw him as a human being who was indeed in a special relationship with God, similar to a prophet, and in this sense a messenger of God, yet not God's physical son. Many of his followers were a part of this movement. The dogma of the Jesus being the son of God was first pronounced as a dogma only in the year 325 at the council of Nicaea. However, this was not so much a result of the shared conviction of the bishops who gathered there, but rather under the massive pressure exerted by Constantine who was the Roman emperor at the time.

Here I would like to explore in more detail the contradictions and inconsistencies of this dogma.

God the father and His son

The first thing is the image of a God father and of a God son.

How can we conceive of this God? Is He a human being? Was he created in the image of a man, for the benefit of the believers? Did He father a son? Was it, for instance, through the Angel Gabriel when he appeared to Mary to tell her in the name of God that she would give birth to a son, without human contribution, without a human father, so that this son would be a Son of God.

This is described in detail in Luke, where Mary said to the angel: "How should this be, as I don't know of any man?" The angel replied to her: "Holy Spirit will come over you and the power of the highest will overshadow you. Therefore the Holy that will spring forth from your womb will be called the Son of God." (Lk.31 – 36)

Here we can mention that the idea of sons of gods was widespread in the Roman Empire at the time of Jesus. Many gods had sons and daughters and they came in disguise when they wanted to make a human woman pregnant, such as Zeus, the father of the gods, who appeared as a swan.

It seemed as if these gods needed a human woman to father demigods, who then came into their father's service as the heroes. The gods revealed themselves to the humans in this indirect way.

That this idea showed up in many myths seems to have a tangible background. There are some pointers that in some dimension and distant past the earth was visited by beings from another planet, and that these visitors bred a new species of humans with the women on the earth at that time. Together with them the visitors founded a highly evolved civilization, the remnants of which we still marvel at today. We cannot imagine how these remnants were possible, given that even in our time with our means we are not able to recreate them, like for instance the Cheops Pyramid.

Zechariah Sitchin explored these questions in his books. Through his discoveries he turned his hypotheses into a scientifically probable fact.

Therefore our ideas of a son of god have a background that reaches far into the past. Looking at it this way, it would be high time that we redeem Jesus from the idea that he is a son of god, as the bible describes him, and that we let Jesus be a human being who failed in the end, abandoned by his god as he had imagined him to be.

The dogma of infallibility

The basic dogma of the church was and still is the dogma of infallibility. All other dogmas are based on it.

To begin with, it was Jesus who was deemed to be infallible, even though, in spite of the sonship of god attributed to him, he is also censured and his teachings are contradicted in the gospels. Examples are found earlier in the chapter: Risen from the Dead.

Second, the bible is held to be infallible, in spite of its contradictions and its images of horror, especially of the apocalypse.

Third, it is the church itself and its traditions that are held to be infallible, even though there were different traditions in the beginning. I am thinking above all of the movement of the Arians who rejected the dogma of Jesus being the Son of God.

In the course of time, the church councils were the institution that decreed bindingly and therefore infallibly which dogmas had to be believed and which ones had to be condemned. Those questioning these doctrines were not only excluded from the church, but also from eternal salvation.

In recent times another aspect of infallibility was added. At the First Council of the Vatican the Pope was declared infallible when he raised a doctrine to the status of dogma. Since then there are two doctrines above all that the Pope pronounced to be dogmas. I will look at this more closely now.

The immaculate conception of Mary

The first one of these dogmas was the dogma of the mother of Jesus' immaculate conception. What is really meant by this most of the believers do not even know. This dogma states that Mary's parents conceived her without original sin. What is meant by original sin, I described in more detail in the chapter "The Beginnings of the Church." Original sin means that from Adam and Eve on, they and their descendants were excluded and have remained excluded from paradise to this day; and therefore also from the mercy of God.

These days many shake their head in perplexity. But this doctrine is a dogma. Those not believing in this dogma are excluded from the church and from eternal salvation. As stated earlier, this is demonstrated most drastically by the fact that children who died before being baptized had to be buried outside of Christian cemeteries. They did not belong to the church and not to Jesus either.

Here I would like to point out some questions and incongruities in the so-called Immaculate Conception. I hope I won't tire you, but because this doctrine is also a dogma, it is crucial to believers.

The question I pose to myself: Were Mary's parents also freed from the original sin before she was conceived? Or was it only Mary? If so, then were Mary's parents still her real parents, or did someone from outside interfere in this parenthood?

The other question is: Why was it foreseeable that Mary would become the mother of Jesus?

Was Jesus also born without original sin? Was he really one of us then? Then what about his brothers and his sisters? By the way, in the gospel of Mark, Jesus' brothers are listed by their names: Jacobus, Josef, Judas, and Simon. In the same place it is also mentioned that Jesus had sisters too. How about Mary's virginity then, if she had a husband and so many children? Of course these questions appear absurd for some. Yet they logically follow from this dogma.

The physical ascension of Mary

Something similar follows from the dogma that up to this day has been the last dogma to be declared infallible by a pope, here by Pius the twelfth. It is about the dogma of the physical ascension of Jesus' mother after her death.

After the comment in the gospel of Mark that Mary stood under Jesus' Cross with John, Jesus' favorite disciple, Mary is not mentioned any more.

By the way, this remark is questionable. The Gospel of John was written last, after the three synoptic gospels, apparently very late, and by someone who was familiar with Greek philosophy. Did the author of this gospel want to identify himself with Jesus' favorite disciple? In the gospel of John, Jesus on the cross says to his mother: "Woman, this is your son," and then he says to the disciple: "This is your mother." From this passage it was concluded that this disciple looked after Jesus' mother later on.

In the earlier gospels we find no reference to this, and nothing about Jesus caring for his mother, but there are passages about how Jesus behaved in a rather reserved way towards his mother and his brothers. Therefore the question comes up: What about Mary's other children and perhaps even grandchildren who may have cared for her?

What I am saying in the chapter "Risen from the dead" about Jesus' resurrection and his ascension equally applies to the physical ascension of Mary.

Here again, the question is: To what kind of a god does she ascend? Does he have a physical body? Does he have a royal household and entourage, like the Greek gods on mount Olympus? After her ascension, does Mary take up the role of a goddess, so that Jesus does not only have a father in heaven, but also a mother? This would explain why in their religious practice people revere Mary as a goddess in many places.

And here, too, those denying this dogma, even though it is full of contradictions, are excluded from the church and therefore from salvation.

As a student of theology I experienced this firsthand.

At that time when the professors of theology debated in the church whether the belief in Mary's ascension could be made a dogma, there was complete consensus amongst them that there was no evidence for this in the bible or in the early Christian tradition.

When this dogma was pronounced regardless, they caved in. For the principle of the pope's infallibility still held true, condensed in the Latin saying: Roma locuta, causa finita. In English: Rome has spoken, the matter is closed.

The infallibility of the Pope

A final thing about infallibility, here concerning the infallibility of the Pope. The question comes up: How does a human being who used to be fallible become infallible? He becomes infallible through being elected as the pope by the enclave of the cardinals.

Who or what makes him infallible? Who or what makes him the representative of Jesus and his god, and therefore infallible? Does Jesus have a say in this? Does God intervene here, or is it done by humans only?

The election of a new pope is of far-reaching consequences for the Catholic believers, and especially for the bishops and priests who must swear an oath of allegiance in order to be allowed to remain in their position, even though Jesus explicitly exhorted his listeners: "You must not swear an oath."

What about other churches? They did not follow these dogmas, with the exception of the dogma of infallibility. They also behave as if infallible, for instance when they publicly slander deviationists and warn others about them. It's different concerning their belief in Jesus and his god. Here they largely remain in conformity with their church of origin.

Final question: Which reforms are possible?

In the same way I could say something similar about all the dogmas that were not discussed here and also those that I discussed in detail in the chapter, "Risen from the dead."

What reveals itself here? The dogmas and doctrines of the doctrinal edifice of the church are myths. Theology is mythology.

On the path of demythologization of some dogmas of the church I have taken you along a fair stretch of the way. From what we have seen, can any attempts to reform the church from within have a future? Can we reform myths? Myths must fall.

Guilt and penance

(Live from the Mexican Congress on Systemic Education, presented to 1.500 participants, predominantly teachers, July 24 – 29, 2012)

Bert Hellinger after a short film about stations of his past.

It was a long road that took me to where I am now. Even though I am supported by many forces of my past, I am looking ahead.

It moves me deeply that so many faces look to me and expect something from me that serves their life. But I am not standing here on my own. I feel connected to greater powers. From there, often quite unexpected, an insight comes to me. Sometimes, when it takes hold of me I begin to shake. The extent of these insights makes me shake. I know what kind of resistance they will meet with. So, I am cautious.

Sometimes I take a small step forward and leave much unsaid, even though I know the dimensions of these insights are overwhelming.

One of these insights – shall I tell you? – concerns the topic of guilt and penance. Yesterday at the dinner table someone asked me: What is the opposite of sin?

I thought about it, and suddenly the answer came to me. I had it in only one word, and I don't know if it is easy to translate. The word is: unique. Said more clearly, this means: Those who know and feel they are free from sin take of God's place.

Those knowing themselves guilty stride safely on earth. They remain on the ground. All greatness is on the ground. Who wants to be higher becomes less.

Now I begin to pause, for I feel what I shall and must say now is monstrous.

To Sophie: You feel how hard this is. Stand by my side.

Sophie stands to the left of him.

These insights we have often shared. We kept on going further and further in this exchange. Sometimes Sophie encouraged me to go further. Sometimes she said: "Pause. This is too powerful. You put yourself into danger if you say this publicly." In this big group I also see this concerning schools and teachers and students.

Now I take a step forward.

Bert Hellinger is at the podium. He takes some steps forward, closer to the audience.

This turned into several steps.

The good conscience

All suffering of the Occident, all wars of the Occident, all suffering that the Occident brought to South America; it all comes from a fundamental idea. "You are guilty!" "You have no right to live." "We are better." "We are innocent when we kill you – in the name of god."

Behind this is my original insight about conscience: About the clear, or good conscience, and about the bad conscience. About the strange idea that is still at work in the Occident, in religion, as well as in public life, in the legal system, and in all wars: "My good conscience is the voice of God in me." I must therefore follow this conscience.

Get a sense inside yourselves whenever you think you must follow your good conscience, what are you doing? You reject someone. Every rejection comes from the good conscience. Rejecting someone means referring to the voice of one's good conscience, to one's God.

Now I am looking at the schoolteachers. When they reject someone or give someone preferential treatment, they feel in harmony with a greater power. Strangely, the more they reject or even harm someone, the stronger they feel.

Can you resonate with that?

When I renounce the voice of my conscience, when I renounce my good conscience, and my arrogation that comes along with my good conscience, then what do I see in the other? What do I see in the student? What do I see in the student's parents? What do I see in what the student or the parents are doing?

I see their good conscience. So, in the bad things they are prepared to do, they follow their God, and I as a teacher follow mine.

The conflict between me and their parents, for instance, is a holy war. Two different gods are doing battle with each other. What kind of a battle? Always a battle of life and death.

I think I must stop now. Perhaps later on I'll come back to this.

What have I done now? I have taken you into another consciousness, beyond guilt and penance. I have taken you along into another love.

Guilt and penance continued

After a while: I will pick up the topic of guilt and penance once more, including its application at school and in one's personal life. Is that okay with you?

(A loud yes from the audience)

Now I will take a few steps forward again, into the public arena as it were, and I come back to guilt.

Penance

The image of guilt is like a knout in the hands of those wanting to submit humanity to their will.

What happens to a child when a mother says: "You are bad." Is he still a child? Is she still fully alive? Or does he sag inside, losing the contact with the world and with the love of other people? Even the contact to her parents? Is the mother still the mother for this child? Is the father still the father for the child? How does the child respond then?

An inner movement begins in the child, an attempt to get rid of the guilt. We call this movement penance.

What does the child do when he wants to get rid of the guilt in this way? He harms itself. How does the child harm himself?

The child does something to himself that leads into death. Can you feel that? Is there anything more hostile to life than this idea of guilt and penance?

I have trouble continuing with this. The consequences are incredible. The whole Christian Occident is held in bondage by an institution that gains its power from the idea of guilt and penance. This institution is called church.

Jesus on the cross, and God

Imagine this: Jesus is on Mount of Olives and he prays to his father in heaven: "Let this chalice pass me." What was the chalice? His death on the cross. Then he says: "Not my will, but yours will be done."

Who nailed Jesus to the cross? Did the hangmen do it? Was it the Roman prefect? It was God his father. He wanted this death.

Then Jesus cried out on the cross, naturally: "My God, my God, why have you forsaken me!"

What kind of an idea is at work behind this monstrous process? Why should Jesus die on the cross? Why should the Son of God, as he was called later, die on the cross?

Because this god felt offended, and he could only be appeased through his son's death on the cross.

Can there be a more horrible god? A more inhuman god?

Later on the Christians relentlessly tried to appease this god. Every holy Mass in which even the pope holds up the host is a reenactment of the sacrifice on the cross. During Mass the Christians receive the communion as the body of Jesus. They are supposed to eat it, like cannibals eat human flesh, in order to be redeemed through this act.

Then the chalice containing the blood of Jesus is given to them to drink. The believers agree and hope to be redeemed from their sinful actions, from their guilt. With this image even children are kept at bay and subdued.

The other redemption

From whom do we need redemption? Do we need redemption from our guilt? Do even the little children need it, so that they shall be redeemed from their guilt through being baptized, and without baptism they cannot go to heaven? From whom do we need redemption?

We need redemption from this terrible god. We need redemption from this idea of guilt that entails eternal hell, and from our attempts to pay for our sins through penance.

I went out on a limb here. How can I? I have put the fear of this god aside.

The other consciousness

Now let us get back to guilt. And back to school. What would be the greatest service to these children who are sitting in front of us in their classrooms? To help them make the transition into this other consciousness, beyond innocence and guilt, and beyond the attempt to free oneself from guilt through self-punishment. This would be a revolution, the real revolution.

When we look back to the constellation we had this morning, why did this boy want to die? To do penance, of course. But not for his own guilt, but for that of someone else.

There is a sentence that has become essential as the cause of many illnesses, as the cause for much suffering and for death.

This sentence is: "Me for you." The child says this sentence – only deeply inside of course – to one of the parents. To whom did the boy in the constellation say this? He said it to his mother, and the father could save him.

What did the mother say in this constellation? Earlier, internally of course, without being aware of it. She said to him: "You for me." And the son replied: "Me for you."

Meditation: "You for me," "Me for you"

Just close your eyes. We sense inside us. To whom did we perhaps say as parents: "You for me." More precisely we said with this sentence: "Do penance for me." "Die on the cross for me."

Did a child of yours answer you with this sentence: "I for you"? Are we still parents then? Are the children still children? Which god plays the key role here? Which belief? Which fear? Where is life in all this? The full life?

Now we look at this god. We resist him to his face. We look beyond him, into the far distance, at yonder creative power from whom all life comes.

The school

I kept my focus on the school the whole time, and on the teachers and students, each one of us and each one of them individually. Where? Here in my own heart.

Once we have succeeded in stepping into the other consciousness, we also enter another love and another joy, the joy about everything as it is.

The other love

Now close your eyes once more. We look into the eyes of everyone close to us. We say yes to each one of them. This yes comes to me directly from another eternal power. Upon everything we rejected until now, a light shines from afar, a light that says to everything that is inside us: "This light comes from Me. Take it and pass it on."

Then our faces begin to shine. When our children or our students look at us, they feel accepted as they are, loved as they are. What do we have in the end? Pure joy.

Other mythological backgrounds

The Greek myths

I will return to the myths once more. In this I will restrict myself to the cultural sphere of the Occident, and to the myths that influence it to this day, still setting its direction, so this means above all, the Greek myths. These myths were passed on to us most extensively. Externally, their immediate influence largely receded when Roman Christendom seized power.

Yet, remarkably, Christendom is also built on another myth, not dissimilar to some ancient myths, and it still follows it.

But first of all, back to the Greek myths. They recount, above all, the adventures of semi-gods; that means, humans who had a god for a father. It is remarkable that it is practically always a male god creating a semi-divine being with a female human.

The supreme god, Zeus or Jupiter, was constantly busy seeking out human females to produce children with them. Often he tricked the women, appearing in the form of another creature, as a swan, for instance, or some other animal.

Who are these semi-gods after all? It is us, the present-day humans. There are ancient accounts, in the Gilgamesh-Epos, for instance, that tell of beings from another planet who came to earth for a while, to live here and exploit her treasures, especially her gold. As mentioned before, there are stone buildings that could never have been built by humans like us, the pyramids, for instance. The precision with which they were built we could not even achieve today.

Now there are accounts of beings from other planets who came to Earth and sought sexual contact with female ancestors of ours, perhaps also in various disguises. The result was also a human being but not the same as those who descended solely from Earth dwellers. These mixed people looked to someone who came from elsewhere as their father. They looked up to these visitors, as if to gods, and these gods looked down on those who were similar to them, but never the same. They saw these strangers as semi-gods, and these revered ones also felt that way.

Our human civilization, so it appears, came about through the contributions of these gods and semi-gods, and the same goes for the different religions. For these gods, even in the so-called high religions, have human traits, as if they were like humans in many ways. At the same time those who call on these gods and serve them want to be more than just mere humans. They want to become more like these gods.

I am aware that these observations may come as a shock to many, especially if until now they have looked at the Occidental Christendom and other religions as being independent from these myths.

When we look at Christendom in the light of these myths it appears to be a new version of older myths (consider the myths around Krishna), essentially the same as the older ones.

Let us have a look at the so-called virgin birth. Mary was made pregnant by a messenger of God. So she gave birth to a son who had God for his father. This son was a semi-god in the language of myths. He proved that with the many miracles he performed or that were attributed to him.

Later on in organized Christendom he was described as a god-man, as a semi-god.

I continue with these observations. The question is: What happens to his followers who believe in him as a god-man?

They want to become like him. Following him, they want to become god-like, that is, less human and more god.

In this connection the doctrine of the original sin appears in a new light. According to this doctrine, all human beings are imperfect from birth, before this god or these gods. They lack something that only the gods have. Therefore what is needed is a heavenly marriage, to be wed to this god, so that they become more like him. In Christendom this heavenly marriage is baptism.

But this movement and this longing for a heavenly marriage still continue on many other levels.

Those who are truly selected by this god to become like him must renounce earthly marriage. Men have to castrate themselves through a vow of chastity or celibacy, and the brides who are chosen by god call themselves brides of Christ or of God. Everywhere in the myths it is about sex, and often not even in a disguised form. Only through the sexual union with a god did and do semi-gods come about.

It is always a human who wants to become godlike. Remaining in this mythical context, what does god want? He wants sex, especially with a woman. Who can be present at such an event? Only an emasculated man. Therefore, in organized Christendom only emasculated men are allowed to serve god, with few exceptions. Therefore, those who are chosen by him or who feel chosen and behave accordingly, nearly all remain without a woman. Only god may touch and take them. He alone may lay his hands upon them.

So, in the light of these observations, what is organized Christendom and some other religions? What are they about? May I dare say it? What are their adherents and chosen ones seeking? They seek the sexual union with a god so that, with his help, they can become semi-gods.

Religions beyond myths

In the sphere of myths, many humans treat their god or their gods as though they were the same as humans in many regards. They praise them, fear their jealousy, and want to be with them in their lands, to live there with them, happily ever after.

These ideas suggest that this god and these gods are similar to humans, that humans and their gods belong to the same species, so that humans are flesh and blood of their flesh and blood. They point out that humans are in the service of this god or these gods, and they must take care that the gods are well and have enough nourishment, such as animal and human sacrifices, for the gods delight in their aromatic smell.

These images are rooted in a reality as the myths portray it. Which reality? That extraterrestrial beings came to visit the earth and together with the ancient inhabitants procreated modern humans, according to their image as it were, and in their service and their lust.

Therefore, the believers of established religions behave as if they were chosen by their god and their gods, as if blood-related, as if they came from another planet also, to make the earth subservient to their wishes and to exploit it.

I have described this in a fairly radical way. But can we really put it more mildly?

The question that might come up here is: Where does this god come from, where do these gods come from? Do they also have a god? Is there a universal power in whose service they are?

When we also consider this we catch our breath. What about our myths of being chosen, of being children of god? Do we become small in the face of these powers? The same as everything else in the world? Called into being and held in being by the same power, creatively new in every moment?

Can this creative energy have a human face and feel with us in a human way? Could it be for us or against us, for example?

What are religions before this power then? Are they not null and void?

But still, we feel this universal energy flow through us at any moment, all of us thought and wanted by it, as we are, without good and bad, all equally held in life by its energy. Enduringly held by it in life and in existence, in this sense, like this creative energy and power, without beginning, without end.

Taken by this universal energy, how do we live on earth then? Can we still exploit it? Or do we humbly fit in, at one with everything?

What about religion then? Do we still need one? Does life require a heaven or even a hell, or the love of god and the fear of god? Are we not at all times at one with this universal energy and power, accomplished and moved by it alone?

Have I risen above others with these thoughts, and above their religions? Are they not also wanted by the same energy and also in its service?

So I withdraw from these thoughts, aware of my limitations in every way, and I humbly take my place in something greater.

In what? In the moment now.

The first mover

Aristotle speaks of this idea of a first mover, a first mover who moves everything because he thinks it. So everything there is owes its existence and its movement to the thinking of an all-pervading spirit. From this follows the idea that this spirit not only thought everything, as it moves, but also keeps on thinking it in its every movement. Looking at it this way, we perceive this spirit and this first mover immediately at work in everything that moves and how it moves.

Yet we observe the experiences that we have with inner images, for instance that we are free to expand restricting images into images with new possibilities, and thereby achieve something in one way or another. In light of this we may have to look at the movement that originates from the first mover in a sense that is infinite and vast, and understand it that way. This means, it is rather in accord with our experience that there is room to move for us in what the first mover moved, so that we can learn and create new things, including making mistakes, taking wrong paths and witnessing failure that comes along with these.

In this way, in spite of our basic dependence on this other movement, we still make our own luck. In which way? Through our thinking, through our experiences, through our aims, through our narrow or broad consciousness.

Yet in everything we can think and experience, we think and feel in relatedness to many other people, and thus our creative thinking develops together with many others. So our creative thinking develops in the interchange within an all-encompassing human consciousness, taking and giving at once.

Nevertheless it still develops in our dependence on this first creative movement, within its vast all-embracing and interweaving consciousness, in a twofold way, still seen from its origin and its beginning, and also in every moment, carried, accompanied and guided by it.

This shows in the experience that sometimes we feel we are seized by a movement and are taken into its possession, as if it were coming from outside beyond our personal will and wishes. Above all it shows when a new insight is given to us in such a movement, expanding our consciousness as well as that of humanity.

Here the first mover shows that ultimately everything is in his hands.

We are shown something else here. We can also wait for this movement; sometimes even ask for it, preparing ourselves for it internally, trusting it, and as soon as it shows up, following it unconditionally.

Perhaps this all-thinking and all-initiating spirit plays with our freedom, and also with our consciousness, with our images, fears, and wishes. How do we join in then? In passing, waiting, in surrender to the whole movement until it connects us enduringly with its beginning and its end.

The gods

There are legions of gods. They wrestle with each other for supremacy, trying to destroy other gods beside them. Each of these god's demands of his followers: "You shall not have other gods apart from me!"

The god of a man for instance, says this to the god of his wife, and the wife's god says it to her husband's god. The fundamental conflicts between a couple are ultimately conflicts between their gods.

Which means does a particular god employ to assert himself against some other god? Which voice is he using? Which particular voice? We hear the voice of our own particular god through our conscience.

When we heed his voice through our conscience, he rewards us. Then we have a good conscience, and we feel in the right and innocent. When we act against his voice, he summons us to appear in his court via the same conscience. Then we feel guilty and we fear his wrath.

Often there are several people who heed the same conscience. They fear the same god, as they have the same god in common.

So just as there are different consciences, there are also different gods. The gods we fear are above all the punishing gods. Their reward we experience mostly when they release us from their punishment.

In this sense we all have a personal god and also one we share with others, one we fear, together with others. We revere this god with fear and trepidation, in the hope of escaping his damnation.

The shared god is also a limited god. His territory borders the territory of other gods where our god must halt. Whilst some individual gods do attempt to extend their territory, so far none of these gods has succeeded in gaining a worldwide empire over all people, no matter how horrendous and bloody their battles waged against each other have been and still are.

How do we escape the domination of our god and the domination of other gods? Can we succeed in this within our present consciousness and within our different consciences? This world and its consciousness still remain within the service of many gods.

By the way, these gods all share the same name: They all bear the name "I". Therefore the god of the Jews and the god of the Christians called himself: "I am that I am," Yahweh or Jehovah in Hebrew.

The question is: Has this god, and have other gods not achieved great things? Their followers would say so. There is no doubt about that.

But how did those fare who worshipped another god? How much suffering and death did our god bring to them?

The other question is: How do we escape the demands of these gods and the domination of our god?

We just leave our god and the other gods to their ways, as they are. This means, we leave their territory and go beyond the voices of these gods in ourselves, that means also beyond the voices of their many different consciences. We let another consciousness take us along, the consciousness that silences these voices, and also their gods themselves.

When this consciousness takes us along we become still. We experience ourselves in deep unison with everything there is, as it is. We transcend the boundaries of our self, and also of our god's self, and therefore the boundaries of man and woman and the boundaries of heaven and hell and of innocence and guilt.

How do we live then? We live in accord with everything as it is. In the first instance, with ourselves as we are. We live in accord with our past and with our future. We live in accord with all who belonged to us and still do. We live in accord with the living and the dead.

In everything there ever was and in everything that is and will be, we breathe and move in the same rhythm, in a creative rhythm. We are taken along by the creative movement that brought everything into existence with its thinking and willing, continually holding it in existence, even the old gods. But beyond their voices in our conscience they remain transient like everything else. They remain transient as we do. We are lit up by another sun and by another consciousness. We return to our source as we are, with everything as it is and was, at once.

Do we come back again into this life from this experience? We return different, changed.

How? We return with another love, with another consciousness, with a creative consciousness, at one with something ultimate, self-less.

Rome

Rome was once the center of the known world of the Occident, and a center of a so-called empire of peace that lasted for more than 300 years. Under the name of Pax Romana, Roman peace, many people were brought together. Earlier on, these nations and tribes were subjugated by Rome in many bloody battles, and annexed into the Roman Empire.

The peoples of the Roman Empire were all subjected to the same cult, the emperor cult. This means, the emperor was worshipped like a god, sacrifices were presented to him, to secure his blessings and his favor, his benevolence. In this empire of Roman peace, everything revolved around Rome and its emperor.

This empire of peace exists to this day, even if under another name. It is also held together by a cult, not dissimilar to the emperor cult. To this day, remaining in the language of the Roman emperors, the new emperor gives his blessings "Urbi et orbi," to the city and the whole orb of the earth. Even though all the emperors died a long time ago, here they are still alive.

Rome's aura endures, as if the Roman Empire had been resurrected again after its downfall. Now it connects peaceful pilgrims from all over our world.

Can we eschew its spell? It still holds a magic attraction. An unquenched longing in humanity's soul keeps it alive, a dream not yet fulfilled, the dream of a stable benevolent center, taking care of all people, one blessing hand above us all, and we, so small before it, and it, so large it is holding us all.

Their end to meet they rush

In Richard Wagner's "opera", The Rhine Gold, Loge, the semi-god of fire, sings about the gods who enter Walhalla across a rainbow bridge, certain of their dominion and power. Later, in the "Twilight of the Gods" (Götterdämmerung), Loge sends them up in flames to perish, and he sings about the gods: "Their end to meet, they rush, those who deem themselves so strong remaining in their power."

This sentence applies to every tragedy and its heroes: "Their end to meet they rush." Those who want to stay on top in order to preserve their power and their influence walk the same path with all others in the end.

Those who stay down cannot go under. Only when it is a matter of power over others do we safely rush towards their and our end. When we keep the end in view right from the beginning, we reach the end like everyone else, but without falling. Only the gods fall prey to the twilight of the gods.

The same goes for ruling and serving. Those who want to win at all costs will also lose. Those who serve remain on par with all others, on the ground. At the same time those on the ground eschew comparison. Remaining fairly inconspicuous, they do not attract enemies, and thus they are not disturbed by them.

How do we succeed in staying in dignified humility? In harmony with a love that turns to everyone and everything equally. This love is there without drawing attention. It can neither gain nor lose, for it always remains open. It is always overflowing.

This love flows downwards and onwards, like water. There is no return-flow. It renews itself from other sources, from creative powers, always new, without safeguarding measures.

The end of life is the same for all, whether it is a sudden perishing or a gentle transition, whether it comes violently or peacefully, whether it comes in terror or in fulfillment. In the end all the dead are removed from the grasp of the living.

And yet, those remaining breathe a sigh of relief when a mighty or happy one falls, for life is only mighty for as long as it stays.

Where does the divine dwell? It dwells in the depth, in the unfathomable depth. We all fall into this depth.

The priests

According to a widely held image, priests are in the service of God. They pronounce God's will. The believers feel God is present in the priests.

Conversely, the priests are in the service of their followers. They step before God on behalf of them. They ask for God's blessings and they return with God's instructions and commandments.

So the priests stand between their god and his believers. Therefore, as a rule, the believers only have access to their god via a priest. Their god does not speak to his believers directly; he speaks to them through the priests.

The mystic movements seek a direct contact to God and hope to find their personal access to the deep secrets. They are therefore a thorn in the side of the flesh of the established religions and their priests. The mystics move beyond them, with no need of the priests' mediation services, without fear of them, and independent.

Another role of the priests was and still is to make offerings to God.

At first, there were human sacrifices, especially child sacrifices, to reconcile God with them, to keep God on their side.

Later on, animals served as the replacement for humans. They were slaughtered and burned on an altar, or roasted, as a nourishing and pleasing smell for their god. With the help of the sacrifice, their god was kept alive in their view. One can assume that the same was the case with the sacrificed humans. These sacrifices only make sense this way. Behind this is an image of God as a cannibal.

Eventually, this image appeared too cruel, and it was overlaid with other ideas and pushed into the background, for instance, through a form of sacrifice that seems the furthest removed from the original human sacrifice, the sacrifice of the Mass. Here the original flesh and blood are hidden in the form of bread and wine. Who is being sacrificed to God by the priests? His own son.

The Christian priests offer God the sacrifice of his so-called beloved son.

This is not all there is to this image. Originally when a sacrifice was offered to God, it was only partly burned, except in the burnt sacrifices, in the Holocaust.

A part of it, often the best part, was put aside for the priests to consume, and another part for those who had paid for the sacrifices, and for whom the priests had performed the sacrifice.

At these sacrifices everyone sat at the same table with God. They ate the same meat and drank the same blood with God.

In the sacrifice of Mass the same happens. All sit at the table with God. They eat the flesh of his son with him, and in their imagination they become one with him.

What would happen to us if there were no more priests?

There would be no more sacrifices; there would be no more human sacrifices, and no more – barely hidden – cannibalism shared with god. There would be no more priests who fall victim to their god themselves, for instance, through the celibacy imposed on them by the Catholic Church.

In ancient times, in the service of the mother goddess, her priests emasculated themselves in some form of trance, as a sacrifice for her. Celibacy is a sublimated form of emasculation. These priests, putting it very bluntly, yet also precisely, offered sacrifices and were sacrificed themselves.

Can these priests have compassion? Or do they have to become cruel where it matters to be cruel, like the god they serve?

There's something else to think about here. Which god do these priests serve through their celibacy? Is this god a man, is it our father as Jesus called him, or did a mother goddess usurp his place? What is the veneration of Maria, the so-called mother of god, other than the veneration of a mother goddess? Especially where celibacy was demanded of priests, she largely took the first place in the consciousness of the believers. Yet looking at it closely, for the priests the mother goddess is the church. Therefore only men can become priests in it, emasculated men.

How do we bid our farewell to this god and his priests?

First, without fear of this god and his goddess and her priests.

Second, with love for life, as it is given to each one of us, from a power before whom everything has its pure origin to an equal extent, from a power that is above everything and neither needs nor wants sacrifices.

Third, in the devotion to life as it is given to each one of us, directly by this power that keeps our life in existence in any moment.

Fourth, in the love for everything and everyone, including the believers and the priests, without wanting to be bigger than them, as they are also loved by this power like everyone else.

Fifth, humbly so, for whatever we think of this power, whichever way we address it, our ways remain insufficient and limited.

Yet the way we conceive and revere this power makes a difference to our relationships with everything as it is, especially to other people.

Which difference? This thinking and this reverence serve peace and reconciliation with all, without sacrifice and without priests. They serve peace and reconciliation with that hidden God. He is at work in everything with a love that creatively overcomes the distinctions we have set. This love is kindly turned to everyone, without sacrifice, without priests, in every human being's heart, present in an all-embracing love, with him and everything as it is, at one with love.

What this change demands from us, I have sought to describe in a story:

The other God

A man dreamt at night that he had heard the voice of god that said to him: "Get up, take your only son, your only, beloved son, take him to the mountain that I will show you, and there sacrifice to me!"

In the morning the man got up, looked at his son, his only, beloved son, looked at his wife, the child's mother, and looked at his god. He took the child and led him up the mountain, built an altar, tied his hands, drew his knife and wanted to slaughter him. But then he heard another voice, and instead of his son, he slaughtered a sheep.

How does the son look at his father?
How does the father look at his son?
How does his wife look at the man?
How does the man look at his wife?
How do they look at god?
And how does God – if he exists –
look at them?

There was another man who also dreamt at night that he had heard the voice of god that said to him: "Get up, take your only son, your only, beloved son, take him to the mountain that I will show you, and there sacrifice to me!"

In the morning the man got up, looked at his son, his only, beloved son, looked at his wife, the child's mother, and looked at his god. He disobeyed the instruction directly, saying: "I'm not doing that!"

How does the son look at his father?
How does the father look at his son?
How does his wife look at the man?
How does the man look at his wife?
How do they look at god?
And how does God – if he exists –
look at them?

Child sacrifices

Long before the Israelite tribes invaded Canaan and took possession of it, there was a widespread religious belief that parents secured their life and their future through sacrificing one of their children to their god. This was usually the first-born child.

The original sacred site in which these children were sacrificed is now accessible after careful excavations. In the center there is a massive altar made of rock, where obviously several children were sacrificed and burnt at the same time. I went around this altar and thought of these children with love.

Does this testimonial of history, long before the invasion of the Israelites, also remind us of Jesus' sacrificial death on the cross, in honor of his father in heaven? Here within the church there is also the imagination that all who believe in him will be redeemed from their sins through his death on the cross, because god is reconciled with us through this slaughter sacrifice, and we were reassured of his mercy?

Here I rushed ahead of myself. Earlier on, after the invasion, it was also the custom among the Israelites to sacrifice their firstborn to a god. This god was called Moloch. Close to Jerusalem he had a temple. There was a statue of him in the shape of an oven. This is where the parents brought their firstborn children – perhaps it was always the firstborn son – and they threw them into the fire of this god's oven, singing loudly. This was supposed to drown out the screaming of their children.

Many prophets railed against this cult, but it was still kept up for a long time, all the way to the end of Jerusalem through the Babylonian conquest.

The question is: Does this cult also exist amongst Christians? Obviously yes, disguised as a pious rite. The pious Christians say that they dedicate a child to god, here also with the idea that this will invoke god's blessing on them.

Now I come back to the usual forms of dedicating a child to god. Here the virgins who are consecrated to god even appear as brides of Christ and are consecrated to god in a holy wedding. Yet this also means renouncing an earthly bridegroom and children of one's own. But the parents were still proud of these children, for after all, through their sacrifice they brought their parents god's blessing.

Something similar applies to sons who were prepared to join an order, especially for those who became priests. They also had to renounce marriage for the greater honor of god, in order to be there for God alone, as god was – this was the imagination – especially pleased with them – and with their family.

These sacrifices, compared to the earlier child sacrifices, may not be bloody, just as the sacrament of Mass is not bloody, yet the bloody death of Jesus is referred to again and again. But even these sacrifices demand the ultimate from the sacrificed.

Here I restricted myself to the church. Yet this idea of human sacrifices has its effect in other spheres as well, and they are sometimes bloody.

When German soldiers went to battle, they sang this song:

Germany see us, we dedicate
to you our death as smallest action.
When he comes to greet our ranks
We shall become the great seed.

Which myths are still at work here? Are we immune to them? Here, too, the farewell is badly needed and a de-mythologizing that works at a great depth. If we succeed in this, we will also succeed in the farewell to an image of god that wants child sacrifices. And we succeed in the farewell to an image of Jesus that promotes this belief, for instance in the idea that we carry his cross with him.

With this farewell we succeed in the farewell to all gods who for the sake of their magnificence demand human sacrifice, however it may be disguised.

Where do we end up then? We end up beyond the lands of these gods; with another love that neither wants nor needs any sacrifices.

The question still stands: How many sacrifices were we prepared to make, how much renunciation were we prepared to practice, in order to reconcile a god? How many sacrifices and how much renunciation have we demanded of others and imposed on them, to reconcile with our god, and to do what will entice him to be merciful? On which side were we? Were we on both sides?

And thus: How can we free ourselves from this image of god?

We drop it.

How? With love for all and also for ourselves.

God is dead

I hope you are not taken aback reading this heading. As if I were so presumptuous, saying something that no one is entitled to say. I was shocked myself about this heading. But it is based on an experience that I pass on to you here.

We had a seminar in Holland that was mostly about the movements that lead to success in organizations. A participant wanted to experience for himself and also generally what would come to light when we look at the church as an organization. He had in mind that through family constellations one could get some understanding of which movements reveal the church's power and powerlessness.

In family constellations something is set into motion through the representatives, who have no influence on it. They experience themselves taken along by other powers that take them beyond their wishes and fears, into insights and spheres that were hidden to them before.

I will just recount what went on at the seminar, happening without any words, in pure stillness.

I asked the course leader to choose a woman from amongst the roughly 160 participants to come on to the stage. I said to her: "You represent the organization called church." She came up, stood there and looked to the front.

After a while I asked the leader to also choose a man from the participants. As he came on the stage, I said to him: "You represent Jesus."

As I mentioned before, everything regarding the representatives took place without words. They allowed themselves to be guided from elsewhere and they followed the inner movements.

For a short time the representative of Jesus stood opposite the church at some distance. Then he turned away from the church, to the right, but not too far, and he looked in that direction.

Then I asked the course leader to choose another man from the audience, a representative for God.

This representative went up the steps to the stage, but only to the last step, without setting foot on the stage. He only looked at Jesus.

Jesus looked at this representative without moving at all. After some time he took two small steps towards God, and then several small steps away from him again.

After another while the representative of God stepped on to the stage. Now Jesus went towards God in very slow and small steps. When he reached God, Jesus and God embraced one another very tenderly and for a long time. Then Jesus released himself from God and moved away from God a long way, yet always backwards, so he could still look at him.

Both still looked at each other for a while. Neither of them had looked at the church at all.

Now some movement entered the church. The church bent forward and looked to the ground. In family constellations this movement shows that someone looks at someone, or perhaps many, dead.

Now I got one more representative, a woman, to lie down on the ground, on her back in front of the church.

The effect of this movement was baffling. God's representative went down to the ground. He knelt beside the dead person. He lowered his head deeply and began to weep.

After a while he lay down next to the dead woman, as if he were also dead.

This was the end of this constellation.

Nietzsche once said – this was considered a provocation at the time–"God is dead." This sentence came from a deep insight. And he was shocked most deeply about it, for he was still in the grip of a deep longing for the unknown God.

In this constellation the same thing revealed itself: "God is dead." Of course we cannot interpret this as a verification of this statement. These movements reach too far for this.

Strangely, after this statement many heaved a sigh of relief. Together with the representatives, many of the participants were also taken along elsewhere by an insight and a movement. Where to? Beyond the images of God that the church presents and – as daring as this may appear here – beyond the image of God that Jesus had. Even this god – we must acknowledge and feel it deeply in our soul – he is dead, he was dead for Jesus, and he is for the church.

This god is dead and yet still there. He is there differently. He cried.

Emptiness

I circle round God

In his Book of Hours Rainer Maria Rilke writes in a poem:

I circle round God, the primordial tower,
and I circle for thousands of years,
and still I don't know: Am I a falcon, a storm,
or a great song.

Everything in us circles round something. Our thoughts for instance, our blood, our wishes, our fears, our hopes, our love. Even though we move and sense ourselves amidst all these circles, the center around which we circle remains hidden to us.

Rilke calls this center God. But he does not know Him. He knows himself attracted by Him, without ever reaching Him. What is left for Him after this circling? A great song remains for Him.

The question is: Whom or what do we encircle? What attracts us so that we encircle it? What do we encircle as if it were God for us?

Can what we encircle be like God? Do we form an image as if what we encircle were our true center? Are our circles so small that suddenly our own self stands in this center? Or are these circles large and then become larger and larger still, because they circle around an ultimate and empty center, with love; and in the end, do we stand still in awe? Do we also turn into a song?

When we look at our surrounds and at the world in which we live, what became the center for many, the center around which they are turning? What became the ancient tower around which they circle? What became this tower for us, that draws our gaze towards it? Do we encircle it without finding this center that makes us pause? Are we also letting ourselves be taken into this movement of thousands of years? Did their tower become our tower? Do we even worship it as if it were our center? Can this center be real, so real that it transcends our images and our longing? For how many millennia do we have to encircle this tower until we realize … this tower was built by us?

When this tower breaks down, what happens to our circling? Do we build a new tower that we can encircle? Or do we pause and look at an empty center?

The question is: What comes to its end in this center?

First of all, our images of God disappear – all images of God.

Second, our fears end, and with them our images of guilt and punishment, and of penance and reconciliation.

Third, our images of heaven and hell dissolve, and also of redemption through bloody sacrifices.

Fourth, our arrogance ends, as if we could be better than others, and as if we were allowed and obliged to convert them to our image of God.

What remains for us? What remains is a great song. A shared song, a liberated song, a song of praise for everything as it is and will be. What remains for us is the surrender to a mysterious ultimate that we encircle and that encircles us. How does it encircle us? It encircles us creatively, new in any moment.

Immeasurable

The immeasurable has no name; otherwise it would be measurable and limited. The immeasurable remains nameless.

Nevertheless the immeasurable is perceived. Through what? Through its effect. How is it perceived? It is perceived as infinite, as unfathomable. Without being measurable itself, it is the beginning of all things measurable, as if it also had a beginning. To us, the immeasurable is without beginning, just as it is without name.

So can the immeasurable be like the ten thousand things, as Lao Tse calls them in the Dao De Ching? Or is the immeasurable pure effect, creative effect? So does all existence, all measurable existence, come from an infinite emptiness, beyond all existence, and yet measurable in the immediate, in everything in existence?

What happens to us if we want to try measuring it, as if we could claim to have a hold on it in this way?

We become blind to what really counts. We become blind to our origin. We become blind to our beginning and to our boundaries.

In which other way do we also become blind? We become blind to our future. Where else can our future be, except there where we come from, beyond all existence?

What happens to what we regard and revere as a measurable origin, to which we even give a name and describe, as if it were behaving similarly to us and had to do so? For instance, when we reward the good and ban the bad from our company? Being presumptuous enough to assume that it belongs to us, as if it were on our side, and against others? Yes, even fighting wars against others in its name, thereby extending its empire and its authority, and assuming that it issues commandments for us and prohibitions, everything precisely measurable?

How far have I veered now from the immeasurable, all the way to what is measurable down to the most minute details?

I deviated from the so-called religions into the realm of the homemade immeasurable. Can there be a more far-reaching confusion and presumptuousness than this one?

What have we done to our world with this presumptuousness? What about our humanity? What about our beginning and our end? What about our immeasurability?

We return with devotion to the nameless immeasurable, away from our many names, away from our presumptuousness, and we return to the transient, to what is there for the time being, to our limitations.

What does this mean for our daily life? We look beyond everything near, towards yonder nameless that is present in it, as small as it may appear to us. We remain speechless before its immeasurable vastness – including its immeasurable within us.

Shocked

We feel shocked when some news has hit us right in the heart. The news of the death of a beloved person has this impact, for instance. Deeply shocked, we feel at one with this person and with the other mourners, and we become still.

We also feel shocked when we realize that we were on a path that took us away from others rather than leading us to them. Deeply affected, we turn around and go back to them.

When lovers feel shocked in this way, they turn to each other with greater sensitivity and become more careful.

It can also affect us deeply when we realize how futile much of what we did really was, only to realize in the end that it took something away from us and others, instead of giving them something.

Is our shock deep enough to pause and turn around? Or do we try the same thing again because the turnaround seems to demand too much from us? What is the result? In the end we give up in defeat.

What shocks us most deeply? Having to acknowledge that the belief in God that we had until now reveals itself as null and void.

Where to from here? Whom can we still trust, what can we still believe? How do we find our way back to ourselves?

We return to reason. We return to nature and to our mother earth. We become most deeply moved by her riches and her wealth and her wisdom and affection and care.

Love is what makes us feel the most overwhelmed. Above all, our love for our partner and for our children. Every day we feel ourselves newly touched by this love, by the many ways in which we express our mutual love. This moves our heart most deeply. So many surprises every day, so many tokens of love.

Being touched in this way is a constant experience in many encounters. Be it the sight of a flower and scent of its perfume, or watching children play, or feeling a cat snuggling up to us.

Sometimes we can also feel a bit overwhelmed, so that we rather turn off a bit instead of being taken fully into this intensity. But this way we lose what is offered and given to us so lovingly. So, let us rather stay with our strong feelings and savour them to the full extent. How? With love.

Joy, bright spark of God's creation

Joy needs light. It seeks the light and it becomes light. Joy glows; its eyes sparkle. This joy unites. It makes us forget what separates.

From where does this joy come? Does it come from us? Can it come from us? We experience it like a spark of the divine, like the light of a creative power. It is just that we can safely imagine this divine infinitely greater. Therefore the image of the spark remains with what is near.

It says in the bible that after the six days of creation, God looked at everything He had created, and He found everything to His taste. Wasn't there a sparkle in His eyes?

How does this joy show with us? Our joy is also joy in everything as it is.

When we feel gloomy, that is, without joy, what had happened before? Did we reject something that is there? In us and in others? Did we lose our joy that way?

So we come back to joy, to the joy about everything that is, and we let our eyes sparkle with joy.

To be precise, this joy begins in us and about us. But true joy goes deeper still. It exists because we have a mother and a father.

I imagine that God looks at our parents, the way He made them. How does He express His joy in them? With which spark of divinity? He finds them very good.

Only once we also find our parents good, as they are, then we also find ourselves good, and with that, everything else as well. Here we find the great joy, a joy that sweeps us away. Taken along by it, we take each other's hands and dance the dance of life.

This joy is a spiritual joy, an all-encompassing joy, without ifs and buts. It is pure joy of living and pure happiness.

Renouncing

We speak of renunciation when we give up something that used to have power over us; an addiction, for instance, as soon as we renounce it, we are free for a healthy life.

Some renunciation goes much further, to the extreme of renouncing life itself, as if our life were in the way of something greater.

In the early centuries of Christianity the idea of renunciation was escalating. The pillar saints, for example, spent their whole life standing on a pillar. Behind this renunciation was the idea of becoming like the bodiless angels.

Such renunciations can still be found today in many fields, for instance, with some yogis. There are also people who discipline themselves so intensely that they can live without food.

Which other spheres of life do they also renounce through these renunciations? They renounce human company. They remain alone, unless they create their own community.

These were extreme examples of renunciation. The question is: Do we behave in a similar fashion when we are satisfied with little, even though nature and other people offer us so much?

Many renounce their health and their life through exposing themselves to dangers that can cost them both health and life.

The question is: How do we learn to renounce renunciation? How do we find the strength for that? We find this strength through the joy in everything that serves life and love. We take it as it is given to us. We rejoice in it and share it.

Does that make us special? Or do we become the same as other people, their equals, in the acknowledgment of our needs, in a beautiful way?

Not to be confused with this renunciation is the right measure. It demands a certain renunciation, yet without taking something away. To the contrary. When we renounce wishes that harm rather than serve us we can see that it is in a right measure.

To what above all are our deviations from the right measure connected? They have something to do with a loss that we feel quite painfully. We miss something so much that we seek elsewhere for something else that helps us bear this loss. This loss is felt in our body, and sometimes concerns our health. But above all it is a loss in the sphere of our relationships, above all, of one of our parents. When we can find them again and are able to stay with them, the right measure in the service of our health comes back to us naturally. There is no effort involved in this.

Where else is it a good idea to find the right measure and to abstain? We keep the right measure on the level of the spirit. This means, sometimes we want to know less rather than more. For instance, less of what harms our relationships and our love. We also want to know less about the god we are attached to, and less about his promises and his threats. These threats push many into the kind of renunciation that harms life and love.

What do we call the renunciation that frees us from this god? We call it reason. This renunciation serves recollection, for recollection is also a form of renunciation. At the same time it makes us rich. It is a recollection towards the essential, and therefore a renunciation towards more – towards more insight, towards more involvement in goals through which we find our fullness, in body and soul at once. This fullness is called love.

"Oh life, life, wondrous time"

This is how Rainer Maria Rilke begins a poem. He goes on:

So puzzling and contradictory in extent.
So often heavily, poorly, sneakily spent,
When all at once, in unutterable rhyme,
Like an angel, whose wings release out wide:
Oh beyond all explanation, oh a life time.

Of all the great risks of being one could take,
Can any burn more bright and bold?
We brace against constraints that our limits make,
Yet capture what lies beyond any known fold.
                    (Translation by Erik Bendix)

Life flows through us anew and whole in every moment. We take it for granted that we are alive, so much so, that we think we own life. In that sense we also speak of our life.

How little we own our life; we can see this in the fact that it can be over quite abruptly. All of a sudden it is gone. As it came, so it leaves us. It comes and goes.

The question is: What about our life before, and what about it thereafter? Was it already there, and does it go on?

It was already there in our parents and in our ancestors, and it continues on in our children.

The question is: Does it also continue in us after it has left our body, and we have become lifeless? Asked differently: Was our life there even before our body? Does it continue later, independent of our body? Is life something spiritual that comes and goes, because it comes from elsewhere and it goes elsewhere? Does this life exist independent of our body and beyond it? Above all, does this life exist beyond our self, before and after it? Are our ideas of our life so contradictory that we can't really adhere to any of them? Does our life here remain inexplicable, from its beginning to its end, daring and great, beyond our scope of comprehension, without our being able to hang on to it?

Yet, apart from our own body, our life enlivens and occupies also the field of the group to which we belong. Therefore beyond us, our family as a whole has a life of its own, and beyond the family this also holds true for the nation and language and religion and culture, into which we were born. They were there before us and they will be there after us.

This living field is mightier than our physical life, so that our physical life remains subordinate to it, and may even be sacrificed to it – such as in war.

Plato calls this field the world of ideas. These ideas embody themselves in our physical self as well as in our culture, here used in the widest sense of the word. For Plato, in contrast to our body and its fate, these ideas were eternal.

In this sense, is there an eternal life in which we participate, even after we have blessed the temporal?

The question still remains: Does our self participate in this life? Does it live on in this field? Apparently so. Otherwise our self could not return to catch the attention of the living. Either immediately, when the dead give the living a message or feed on them and harm them, or indirectly, through their insight and their achievements that are still there and in operation after their death? Here we have the great philosophers for instance, and the great thinkers of enlightenment, the great artists and musicians whose works we can easily access nowadays.

A further question would be: Do we sometimes postpone something for later that our life would be willing to give us now and that it also demands? Do we postpone it – within this life now and also to a life after this life – to another incarnation? Do we become poorer this way, instead of living our life fully, right to the edge of our boundaries?

Rilke gives us the answer in his poem:

We brace against constraints that our limits make,
Yet capture what lies beyond any known fold.

Fullness

The true god, yonder infinite power, from where everything has its origin and that holds us in existence in every moment, is a god of abundance. Everything that alleges that this power wants less rather than more, that for instance it prefers poverty to wealth in all its forms, alleges that this power is also poor, that it wants others to remain poor and become poor. It alleges that if we stay poor we see to it that it gets what it is lacking; adoration for instance, praise, penance, suffering, and even a horrible death, such as the death of Jesus on the cross.

Here the signs are all in the reverse. Who usurped the place of that creative power? Who has put this power into a subservient position, as if this power needed them, instead of the other way around?

The question is: How could this distortion of the creative power ever come about? In Judaism and in Christendom it came about through the story of the eviction of the first human couple from paradise.

What was given as the reason for this eviction? They ate from the tree of knowledge. What kind of knowledge was this? They knew the difference between good and bad. At the same time they knew that they were naked. They knew each other as man and woman.

What was the result? They knew each other in a way that the woman was made pregnant by the man. They became creative, and in this sense, equal to the primordial creative power.

Something else happened through their eviction from paradise. They began to cultivate the earth, in this way also coming into accord with the creative power that created them from the beginning as man and woman, according to its image. Only after the so-called "Fall" did they complete the human creation for which god had made them man and woman.

This explains why so many Christians see the great sin in exactly that which makes them creatively one as man and woman. So, renouncing this great sin reconciles them with this great power and lets them be one with it.

Everything is upside down here. Where is the unison with the primordial power whose creative movements continue on endlessly, above all in and through human beings?

So where do we find this unknown god? We find this god in abundance; in the abundance of life, in the fullness of our physical existence, with all the joy and lust it gives us, when we experience this creative power at work in our body in every way. We experience this abundance wherever we succeed in accord with everything else in existence, in creative joy, for instance in the sphere of the spirit, in every great art, in lofty music in all its many forms of expression, in the fullness of new insights about the cosmos. And we always deem ourselves just at the beginning no matter how far we seem to have progressed in all these spheres. Every fullness is just a beginning, including the fullness of the unknown God, wherever it reveals itself to us in an infinite movement. Before this vastness we remain in silent awe. No matter how far-reaching an insight may appear to us, in its infinite movement it always remains as if purely empty.

Reflecting

When we want to understand something more precisely, we take the time to think about it. When it is about the pros and cons of an action, we weigh carefully what we are allowed to do and how far we need to go in this. When we suggested something to someone, after some time we ask this person: Have you thought about it yet? It is generally accepted that before we comment on something and make a decision, we first sleep on it.

Where do we go when we think about something in this way? Have we thought about what goes on in us in this process?

In this kind of reflection we seek to connect with another knowledge, away from the ordinary thinking. We feel this thinking in our belly rather than in our head. So this thinking sits deeper, it is closer to the earth. We feel it is in accord with greater powers and with our life as a whole.

Looking at it more closely, we follow this level of reflection in our feeling more than in our thinking. We check how our thoughts feel to us. Only then do we know what we want and what matters. These feelings can also be deceptive. Sometimes they take off with us. We act without careful consideration, in love for instance, but also in hate. Therefore we must be discerning when it comes to feelings.

The feeling in the pit of our stomach that connects us to the earth is recollected. As it is in tune with the earth's vibrations, it remains well considered. It is in no hurry.

Often it is the first impression, the immediate feeling that proves to be right. Yet even here it is usually better to act only when we are sure.

Often deep-seated fears block the way to action. Through our environment we are exposed to many different taboos. Therefore we ask ourselves sometimes: Are we really allowed to think that? Moreover: Are we really allowed to say this? And more still: Are we allowed to act in line with it? If we break such taboos of thinking, it can happen that we are excluded from the group that is essential for our survival. These prohibitions can even cost us our life. This was the case for many deviationists in former times, for the heretics, so called by the authorities of the Roman Catholic Church. Nowadays, in a more enlightened society, we have freedom of thought, which protects us from this to a large extent. Yet even here, only within certain boundaries. We only need to think about the so-called political correctness. Even here we need to assess how far our reflections are allowed to go, especially publicly expressed reflection.

Still, our thoughts as such are free. But we better reflect first to what extent we may express them and to what extent we may act in accord with them.

Sometimes a sentence slips from our mouth without having passed our reflection. Those hearing it are shocked, and above all we are shocked ourselves. At the same time everyone feels liberated. At last it has been expressed. It is like in the fairy tale The Emperor's New Clothes when the king paraded past the crowd with no clothes on. No one dared to look closely or to say it out loud. Only one little girl declared for all to hear: "But he is naked!"

Who has reflected here, and who has spoken? Another power was at work here, a power that brings even the long denied into the light of day. Thank God.

The heart

Our heart does not sit high; it sits lower than our head. And at the same time it also sits higher than our abdomen, so it's exactly between above and below. Our heart sits in the middle. It connects above and below, right and left, front and back. Our heart beats for everything, it reacts to everything, often even before it appears. Our heart precedes it – it prepares itself for it. Therefore the heart perceives the future, before our other senses have a chance to focus on it.

So where is the center of our perception? We experience it in our heart and together with it. It reaches far beyond any other perception. Our heart is our core in every way.

The question is: How do we find our way to our true core? To our spiritual center? To the center of everything that is, that was, and that will be? We experience this core with our heartbeat in every moment now.

The other question is: Where does the heart of yonder creative power beat, the heart that brought us into existence and keeps us in existence in every moment, knowingly and mightily, together with everything else that was and will be?

The heart of the creative power beats inside us, in our heart, with its love.

How do we live in surrender to it, how in devotion? When does our heart beat in tune with the heart of everything there is?

It beats in accord with it, calmly and deeply, turned to it, however and wherever we experience ourselves taken along with it, with our heart, into its breathing and working.

With this heartbeat we become wide, all-embracing. With this heartbeat our fears come to an end, above all our fears of the future. With this heartbeat we experience ourselves as healthy, as healthy as in the beginning. With this heartbeat we experience ourselves as trusting the creative power behind everything, as we are in unison with our beginning and our end, whichever way it comes to us, in accord with its end for the time being. This eternal heart is beating enduringly.

Enough

Every movement goes towards a destination. Once the destination is reached, this movement settles down, until taken along into the next movement and driven towards a further destination.

So our movements go from enough to enough, from one enough to the next one, provided we remain in accord with the movement that holds everything else in motion at the same time, from one enough to the next, in this sense in a continuous movement.

This movement we experience as a divine movement, without our being able to intervene, except where we try to direct this movement into a direction that serves a self-referring goal, and try to bring this movement into an opposition to a divine one.

However this can only happen on the surface, and at the high price with which the divine movement asserts itself, so that even here we remain subjected to it and in its service.

About what kind of enough is this in the end? It is about the enough of a fulfilled life here. It is about a divine enough.

What about our images of a god whose favor we gain for our own enough, or from whom we escape with our idea of enough, or even stir up against us? For instance through our insufficiencies and through some guilt that is in opposition to him? In what kind of tight boundaries do we think and act when we come from our fears and our ideas of penance? Still, the myths of all religions move within this vicious circle, in the hope of deliverance from the rejection and the wrath of these gods.

The question is: What about the other god? Can we experience him in our movements? Do we have to form images of him so we can meet with him personally, for good or for bad? Does he have a past for us? Does he have a future for us, for instance as a reward or a punishment, or as chosen ones or as condemned ones? How can we imagine the eternal from whence everything comes as it is, that moves everything as it is, and to whom everything remains connected no matter how and or in which direction it moves? How can we take possession of it or try to make it subservient to us? Can it be taken into possession against others or for others?

Yet nearly all religions move within these ideas, as absurd as they must appear.

In the end, where do we end up with our hopes, with our fear, with our images of good and guilt? Where can we leave them?

We leave them beyond the moment now. The moment alone is enough, and we are enough with our heart in the moment, together with all others, kindly turned to everything, completely in unison with ourselves, turned to this moment with love, and also with its emptiness.

So where does it leave me with my ideas of God? Only in the moment, already empty of him, empty in devotion.

"Come you, you last one I acknowledge"

What comes as the last thing, before the end reaches us? Is it a pain? Is it an insight? Is it a writhing or a rebelling? Is it a dance?

Does the last thing announce itself? Or is it there all of a sudden? Does it wait for a long time? Or does it grab us by the hand in a split second, halting our course?

Come you, you last one I acknowledge. I surrender to you, whichever way you touch me and whatever time you choose to take.

I am awaiting you without waiting. My gaze and my desire are still mesmerized by other things that concern me immediately, transiently, as if I had time.

Still, who or what this last one is at this time remains hidden from me. Everything that preceded it is now overtaken by it.

When it is there, am I ready? Or does it come as a surprise to me?

This last one does not need to come. It is always near us, without showing itself. It is a constant companion. It comes with us wherever we go, just at arm's length away from us, without touching us. When it touches us, the transition begins, either a long one or just a short one.

Having known about the last one for a long time already, having experienced a sense of it already in many situations, as a friend and helper, without ever meeting with it face to face, we never move very far from it, no matter what we are doing. We are well acquainted with it

How does our life fare then? It fares with ease, in a recollected calm, whatever comes our way.

Do we participate less in life then? Or do we participate more collectedly, more essentially, in greater expanse, more awake, kindly turned to everything however it comes? Right from the beginning we also perceive its end, without being distracted from what lies ahead of us. We take it in its fullness now.

Yet we take it as something transient, as something that will have passed soon. Nothing ties us, nothing holds us back. Just like this, we are there 'fully open for everything that is coming, including the last.

Can we prepare ourselves for the last? Do we have to prepare for it?

Our full life prepares us most perfectly. All reductions, all renouncing, all resigning are in the way of the fullness that keeps us open for the ultimate and its accomplishment. If we live in this fullness as is appropriate for us here, we are prepared today any time: Come you, you last one I acknowledge, whoever or whatever it will be that completes us.

Something else helps us to be open and composed with a view to this last: The gaze beyond it, towards a power that guides everything whichever way it comes. For this power there is always a beginning, something that takes us further after each end.

Where to remains hidden from us. Yet even in this life we experience ourselves guided by other powers at any moment. We trust they will guide us beyond our last, beyond another beginning, to another fullness, far beyond our present fullness. In unison with it, we are open for our last one in this life, knowing we will be taken elsewhere, though we don't know where.

So where does our prayer go: "Come you, you last one I acknowledge"?

It goes to this beginning, beyond our present life. How? With confidence, already given to it in our last one here, whichever way it comes, even now most deeply at one with it, at one with love.

Beyond

When we speak of beyond, we must ask ourselves: Beyond what? The opposite of beyond is this side. But then we must ask: This side of what?

When we look at the cosmos, to the extent that we experience it and even see it and know about it, can there be a "this side" and "another side," in the sense that the two are separated from each other and one side is preferred to the other? So, can there be a consciousness beyond this side, in the far distance as it were, beyond this side?

Why am I saying this, why do I ponder this? Because it demands a farewell from many images of less and more, and ultimately the farewell to those religions that are trying to drag us away from the earth and from our body, to a level that alienates us from what is closest to us.

All religions seek to take us away from our life here to a life in the beyond, especially by disparaging this life here, and being prepared to sacrifice it to one in the beyond. They seek to create an opposition between turning to this life and to everything that keeps us alive here and serves the passing on of life, and on the other hand the life in the beyond. Some are even trying to replace the life here with the life in the beyond.

Can there be anything more absurd? Nevertheless, these ideas have kept our relationships and us in check in a devastating way.

The question comes up again: What about our consciousness? Where is our consciousness of life? What about the question concerning god? Can it ever receive an answer? Do we have to give it up? Is it the last decisive step that brings us into accord with the here and now in its fullness? Will we ultimately have to give up these ideas completely? Do I have to give them up? What is left for me then? Infinite emptiness remains.

Is this emptiness within our capacity to imagine? Is it beyond it? Is it beyond our experiences? Or is this emptiness an active emptiness, even though intangible?

Can this emptiness be a destination towards which we are moving? Can there be an image for this emptiness, similar to an image of god?

Here I end my attempts to come closer to the ultimate. How? I am also becoming and remaining empty, thinking and feeling this emptiness.

What is the result? I am staying here, only here, with everything that is here. For a while at one with everything that is here. How am I one? In emptiness.

Do I experience myself less? Do I experience myself infinite in a way, infinitely empty? Empty of all thoughts of God, carried by something nameless, carried by emptiness?

The earth

On the ground

When we have been aiming too high, how do we get down again, onto the ground, where real life happens?

We come back down by the hand of our father. He above all must face real life. Only in this way is his family's survival secured. At least this is how it used to be.

But how is it for so many sons these days, when they have to grow up without a father? When the mother has separated from her husband and the children must remain in her sphere, separated from their father to a large extent? Do they remain on the ground? Or do they climb up high because the mother looks to them primarily with pride, instead of looking at the children's father and acknowledging his greatness?

When the sons remain within their mother's sphere and rise up high according to her wishes, are they still in accord with the earth and in her service? Do these sons often experience themselves as detached, and do others see them this way also? Where is their real strength?

The question arises here: Where do we find, and remain within, the consciousness that brings us into accord with the whole, so that we need not offend others and agree with everything as it is and as it comes, becoming one with everything? We find this accord mostly with our father.

When we transfer these observations to the Christian religions, above all to Catholicism, which presents itself as largely carried on by men, where do the fathers have a place here? Are the fathers pushed into the background by the mothers, who take up the first place for the celibate men? We only need to think of the worship of Mother Mary and of the celibacy that is ultimately connected to her. For this religion the father exists mostly as God the Father, as a father without a wife, and therefore not a real father. The real fathers do not have much room next to him. Or does this Father have a wife after all, a Mother Goddess? What we experience as his wife is the church.

How do we return to the fathers after the Christian religion? We come back from heaven, down to earth, from up there down to the ground.

How do the mothers fare in this? They also return to earth, with the fathers, with their husbands and their sons.

How does the earth fare, how does her consciousness fare? Does it become less? Does it become more? Does it connect instead of separating? Does it remain on the ground, together with everything else?

The breath

When we concentrate on the earth in recollection, we experience her as breathing. She breathes out and she breathes in. Everything we perceive in our world as there with us breathes in and out. Sometimes infinitely slowly, as if it were the creative breath of eternity, and yet, after a while, always perceivable, similar to our own breath that constantly releases something and passes it on, to renew itself in a next breath, creatively held in existence through this breath, from far away.

In this sense, the earth breathes and renews herself in her cycle, and so does the sun in the course of its lifespan. Everything we perceive and experience of our cosmos breathes in, often in a timespan of eons, and it breathes out, ultimately forever.

This breath is creative and knowing. Everything in existence breathes in and out with it.

Besides the breath we can experience, with its rhythm of coming and going, does our consciousness also breathe? The consciousness that is near and familiar to us, and yonder consciousness that we experience as infinite?

How can we experience ourselves as taken along by this breath? Often unexpected and all of a sudden, for instance when we are immediately and irresistibly taken by a movement that in hindsight reveals itself as life saving. Did it come at the right time from this breath? Or when an insight suddenly overcomes us, an insight that wipes away our plans and hopes as if in one stroke? An insight that renders our knowledge and our intentions cast to the wind, and our self as well?

Are we still breathing of our own accord? Or do we become irresistibly aware that another power does the breathing here? The breath of another world, of another consciousness?

Can we halt this breath? Where would we land if we tried? This breath is eternal – and it is self-less.

Infinite

In our language we constantly set specific boundaries with our words, even with the word eternal. That way we constantly move within homemade boundaries. This becomes especially clear to us when we speak of a truth.

Yet it shows up clearly that when we define something as true, it means we impose boundary to the truth. Therefore we can also deviate from a truth. We can deny it, and we can fight it, and above all we can fight those deviating from what we deem to be true.

Truths, all truths, are in opposition to the infinite and to what I am attempting to say about the infinite. This is so for any attempt to gain understanding of another consciousness, of a consciousness that reaches far beyond our ordinary consciousness. Therefore you will notice that we are not so much dealing with understanding, but rather with experiences, with experiences that take us to a higher level, such as to the level where our distinctions of good and bad become secondary. Such distinctions are, rather, like manuals for us to navigate among a multitude of options, finding our way for the next step, in order to transcend that step, too.

I will give you an example from this book. In the chapter about the heaven that brings illness, and the earth that heals, I speak about another freedom, a freedom that leads beyond what makes us ill. In this I follow orders that I have recognized as orders of love. Within limited spheres, above all in our relationships, these orders have stood the test in many ways. If we were to refer to these orders beyond the boundaries of our relationships, such as the distinction of right and wrong, can they apply there? Can they apply to something infinite? Can our present consciousness, our finite consciousness, apply to an infinite consciousness? Here, too, with the distinction of right and wrong or good and bad, and even the greater extreme, to just and unjust?

The same applies to this book as a whole. Any attempt to justify one thing and reject another is also out of the question for me here.

When we experience ourselves taken along into another consciousness, we experience ourselves taken along into emptiness, into a movement in which we neither understand nor actively grasp anything. For the infinite, the distinction between being and non-being, of there and not there, remains incomprehensible for us.

Nevertheless, in our sphere we experience the distinction of being and non-being as necessary and therefore there, even though we cannot grasp non-being.

Therefore, does our gaze to this infinite emptiness and our ongoing experience of this being-moved-from-elsewhere without grasping it lead to surrender to this emptiness? Would it be – what all religions long for from the depth – our ultimate support, and empty support?

I will tell you a story about that.

Story: The not
A monk, out on a quest,
approached a merchant in the marketplace
and asked for alms.

The merchant glanced at him, and paused.
As he handed him what he would spare,
he asked him.
"How can it be that you request of me
what you require for your sustenance
and yet you must think of me and

of my way of life that gives it to you
as something lower?"

The monk replied:
"Compared with the Absolute that I pursue
the rest seems small."

The merchant was not satisfied
and presented a second question:
"If such an Absolute exists,
how can it be something
that someone could seek or find
as if lying at the end of some long road?
How can anyone take possession of it
or claim a greater share of it than others?
And how, conversely, if this Absolute exists,
can anyone stray far from it
and be excluded from its will and care?"

The monk replied:
"Only those who are prepared to leave
all that is Here and Now
will ever reach the Absolute."

The merchant thought about it further:
"Assuming that an Absolute exists,
it must be close to everyone,
although concealed in the apparent
and enduring,
just as Absence is concealed in Presence,
and Past and Future in the Here and Now."

"Compared with what exists
that appears to us as limited and fleeting,
the Absent seems infinite,
as do both whence and wither,
compared with Here and Now."

"Yet what is Absent is revealed to us
in what is present,
just as the Whence and Wither are revealed
in the Here and Now."

Like night and death
the Absent holds, unknown to us,
something that is yet to come.
and only briefly
the Absolute illuminates the Present,
like a flash of lightning.
Thus, too, the Absolute draws close to us
in what is close to us
and it illuminates the Now."

By now the monk was also wondering:
"If what you say is true,
what would remain
for me and you?"

The merchant said:
"For a little while,
the Earth would still be ours."

Intervened

There's always something unexpected that intervenes with what we want and plan to do. It forces us to pause and to take an unexpected direction.

The question is: What is it that gets in the way of our plans, even though we had carefully considered the different steps and thought of all eventualities to safeguard our success?

Sometimes we shake our head when all of a sudden something interferes with our planning, barring our way on one hand, and on the other, showing us something we had not taken any notice of but which now demands our attention.

Are we still conscious then? Are we still with our consciousness? Did another consciousness intervene knowingly to take us elsewhere?

What kind of a consciousness is this? Can it be our consciousness, our narrow consciousness? If that were the case, it would not intervene with our consciousness as it was at the time in such an unexpected way. It forces us to do something that saves us from something that could become dangerous for us and then it shows us a way out that safeguards our survival and that of many others who were connected to us and still are.

What am I describing here? I describe how a consciousness far surpassing us, yet so close to us and taken for granted, constantly intervenes in our life's path and determines it.

The question is: Do we take note of these interventions from outside, of life-saving interventions of a creative power far surpassing us, that like a coachman shortens the reins as if we were horses, and then loosens the reins, without our noticing which coach we are pulling in the end and to which destination? Do we simply keep on cantering? Or do we look back now and then, at the coachman who has our reins in his hands, perhaps smiling at us, and who at other times might turn the horses firmly in another direction, to let us know who is in charge, and calling us to order?

Can we assert ourselves against this consciousness and against its will? Our gaze might suffice for a few steps, but this coachman knows where our life's path goes, and with it also the path of the world.

The question is: How do we come into knowing accord with this coachman, into a knowing agreement with his control of the reins? Or does he even give us free rein after a while, shortening the reins only with an inner accord as it were, maybe just with a little wink?

But what if the road gets rocky? Or if it leads past an abyss? Are we looking back fearfully, expecting our coachman to take hold of the reins quite firmly now?

Reined in by him thus, can we ever look back? Or is the way forward the only one left to us?

What is the result of such deliberations and such observation?

We live constantly in this other consciousness. We are constantly taken by the hand and reined in. We constantly experience his caring attention and discipline.

Does this other consciousness also experience how we turn to it? Does it experience our devotion and our blind trust? Can we, do we, remain in accord with it, even where it takes us on paths that frighten us, because we draw his coach on a path that no one else takes? Where there is no one in front of us or by our side? Only here are we purified from our self-referring consciousness. After a while our gaze goes into an endless expanse, which entices us and at the same time demands the ultimate from us – a daring knowing and a daring action.

Then what about our narrowness? What about our fears and worries?

We experience ourselves taken along into another knowing and another way of acting, often beyond what we knew and had at our disposal until then. Often also a lonesome knowing and a lonesome course of action, and yet in accord with a creative power that is kindly disposed towards everything. In accord with it and at peace.

Despair and discord

The word de-spair contains the "de," away from something, in this word, separated from hope – and dis-cord tells us that hearts are not at one. There are two sides that cannot join, because they push away from each other, into opposite directions.

What is the result? We have no path on which to continue, neither in the one nor in the other direction.

When we can't make any headway, neither in one nor in the other direction, how do we feel after some time? De-sperate. We are without hope.

What would be the solution? How do we escape the dilemma of the equal attraction in two different directions?

We find our way back to a point where they become one again. Though from the outside it may appear as three, a third way, that is father, mother, child. But looking at this apparent three is a new one, in which the "de," the separations of two, join into a union. With this new "one" the de-spair and the dis-cord come to an end.

So what makes us despair? The two that has lost its union. It has lost the concord to return to its shared origin, as well as the concord in a forward movement, in which the "dis-cord" of separation can return to a "con-cord," a union of one-ness.

So who above else is dis-couraged? The child without the parents, the man without his wife, the woman without her husband.

Are we also dis-couraged concerning God? Do we want to be with him, but can't?

The question is: Whom does God represent for us? Perhaps the missing mother or the missing father? Does He represent, as is often the case with those who want to reach God through renunciations, the missing partner in life? Is God still the shared origin of everything there is? Have we dis-connected Him from the shared origin of all existence? Is this the cause of our dis-couragement?

The question is: How do we undo the "dis" between Him and us? We return from the discord to arrive at the con-cord that joins us all, and thus we do away with separations between us, and between God and us, in every way.

Peaceful

Sometimes we come into a room full of people, and we are amazed by how peaceful the whole atmosphere is. Immediately something restless drops from our shoulders. We pause, we calm down, and we breathe deeply.

We feel good here. The opposites appear to have reconciled. Everything is allowed to be as it is. Everyone and everything may be as it is, including what is in us. Even our mistakes. Do we still experience them as mistakes? Do we experience them as mistakes in others? They are a part of our fullness.

Peaceful also means multifaceted. Instead of evening the differences out, or wanting to get rid of them, they are allowed to be there and to unfold. They meet in harmony and work together, inside us, in others, and between us. At the same time we observe our limitations, neither doing away with them nor going too far. Peaceful, we contain ourselves.

Having become peaceful inside, we radiate peace. People who feel they have to get away from each other ask our help so that they can come together again or go their own way peacefully.

The end of war is always marked by peace. Only peace can last. Wherever we go to do battle in whichever way, the battle and the conflict can only end when it is followed by peace. Peace is the result of the exhaustion on both sides. Peace is won through exhaustion. Powerlessness wins the battle for peace.

Peace is therefore a matter of boundaries. Both sides have come to some boundaries where they must halt. Why? Sheer exhaustion. The exhaustion and the losses pave the way for peace. Can the timely insight into these boundaries prepare and help achieve peace? Obviously not.

What do these observations show us? Peace lies in other hands, surpassing our reason. Above all, these other hands surpass the self. Only the self wants war. Only the self wants victory and the submission of the other side.

With what kind of a self are we dealing here? Is it our personal self? It is mostly a group-self. Conflict of this scale is about the expansion of our group-self and about survival of the group with which we have become one.

What brings peace after a conflict? Two different group-selves become one Us. The keyword for peace is therefore: Us.

What I said about the outer peace applies first of all to the inner peace. Opposites come together in us and become one. Body and spirit for instance, or right and left, above and below, male and female, past and the future, life and death.

This also holds true for our relationships, above all in the relationship that is most important to us, between man and woman.

Both man and woman belong to a group-self. Both are embedded in their background, in the immediate and in the wider sense. Both are loyal to their origin, therefore they come into a contrariety that attracts them on the one hand and causes conflict on the other.

How do they overcome what turns them against each other even though the same thing also attracts them so strongly?

They grow into a new Us, into a peaceful Us. Just like their bodies become one, they also become one in their group-Us. Where most of all? In their children.

Peace remains our highest goal. Peace with everything as it is, and ultimately the peace with our source.

What do we find wherever we achieve peace? We find our way to fullness, to the fullness of our happiness.

The spirit

We constantly distinguish between body and spirit, often in the sense that assumes the spirit is higher, on a superior level, and the body is in its service. Therefore we often neglect our body, feeling superior to it and even going against it, for instance through dramatic renunciation. Or we expose our body to danger for goals that are outside of its scope, that appear more important to us, willing to sacrifice its well-being to something beyond it.

Something similar applies when we speak of our consciousness, especially of a higher consciousness. With this idea we put ourselves above our body and above everything that creatively serves its survival through renewing it and letting its wounds heal. Is there anything in our spirit, mighty as it may appear, that can be compared with this spiritual achievement? Can there be anything more absurd and devoid of spirit than the attitude that wants to place the body into the service of the spirit? Through renunciation for instance? In which light do many spiritual paths appear here, and with them, many religions? Where is the spirit in this attitude? Where is, greater, the other comprehensive consciousness? Where is the consciousness of the earth? Where is the father? What is in tune with the greater here?

Does the decisive progress not consist in the return to the origin, the return to the earth and to those powers that uphold all in its existence? How different would life be? How different would the earth be? How different would love be, and the love for life?

Here I would like to turn your attention to an image that we have largely pushed into the background, with a view to the spirit and to an all-embracing consciousness. It is the image and the meaning of our father.

A father is more than a man. Therefore it is not appropriate to contrast what I will say about the father with a woman, but instead, with the mother.

The mother is inclined to draw the child towards her, especially a son, and this means, away from the father. From what does she also draw the child away? She draws her child away from the earth and therefore most directly from the creative spirit that immediately keeps the earth in existence, alive in every moment, and everything that lives on it and is there at the same time. Spirit as we predominantly imagine it to be is in contrast to the earth and everything that thrives on her. Therefore, with spirit we rather associate something that surpasses the earth and all existence on her. Therefore, many, and above all the religions, locate spirit in a sphere beyond the earth and the body, in a so-called supernatural sphere, with all the consequences that result from this idea, in our attitude to the earth and to our body.

Something similar happens when we speak of a higher consciousness, of a different future consciousness that overcomes and surpasses our so-called past and more narrow consciousness. This path is sought above all by the sons whom their mother removes from their father's influence, because she has some so-called higher purpose in mind for them and wants to prepare them for it.

The father, on the other hand, sees his life above all in the service of his children's and their mother's survival, and therefore neglects everything else and must do so. Thus he must remain in the service of the earth and in the service of earthly progress, in the service of earth's spirit. It is therefore imaginable for a father to renounce the earth? To renounce the earth and life on her, as if they are or were in second or last place? Seen from this point of view, where does the future of the earth and the life on her lie? In which other attitude and in which other consciousness? Where do we find the actions that are aware of their responsibility? Where do we find the spirit that we can experience immediately in every existence inside us and at work in our world in a saving and healing way?

We can also ask: Where do we find God? Where and how do we experience ourselves as spiritual and religious in a complete way? And, how do we find our way back to this spiritual consciousness? We find our way back in accord with our father.

The formula

Which formula keeps the world together? According to which formula does it come about or vanish? According to which formula did we develop? According to which formula do we vanish and rise again differently and new in constant change?

The formula is: Out and in, rising and vanishing, and the reverse. In vanishing something rises, and in rising something passes, so that one is inextricably interwoven with the other.

Every rising turns into vanishing, and every vanishing prepares the next rising, without finishing in what is coming.

Are there any exceptions? Can something be both one and the other in one breath, vanishing and rising at once? Do we rise through vanishing, and do we vanish in rising, are both together a single continuous process?

For instance, do we become more through vanishing, and less through rising, and also more, at once? Is there anything that joins both into a union? Is there a consciousness in which the two remain a one, the before and the after, the vanishing and coming, an eternal now? Do we eschew the course of time in accord with this consciousness and keep on being there and here with it infinitely?

By now you might ask yourself where I am taking you with this thought. Is there anything left that endures? Is there any remaining existence, without coming and going, something beyond all being, something that was before it and will still be there after it? Does this also apply to every religion and to every god? Could this ultimately apply to us as well?

We have a formula for this word. Everyone understands it without grasping it, for it is an eternal word, unfathomable and yet there with any other word. This word is: Not.

Whenever we think anything, we also think this word, without grasping it. In every coming and passing we also think it. It becomes the basic formula of all knowledge and the basic formula behind everything that comes. Behind all existence that we can only imagine as changing, it remains, as absurd as it may appear in the moment, the enduring.

Is there a position in which we come into accord with this not? I have endeavoured to fathom it in a story. It is called:

Fullness

A youth asked an old man
"What is the difference between us,
you whose life is almost over
and me whose life is all ahead?"

The old man replied:
"I have been more.
True, the new day as it dawns
appears to be
more than the old day that has been,
because that day has passed.
Yet, in the process of unfolding,
the new day can only be
as it already was -
and it becomes more,
the more it has been.

And like the old day
it too will rise steeply at first

towards its zenith at noon
and seem to hang there a while
at its peak
before sinking ever further and deeper
into the west,
drawn by his increasing weight,
becoming whole
only as it
is completed.

Still, what has already been
is not lost.
It remains
because it was once,
influences
although its time is past,
and is increased
by what is new.
It is like a saturated drop
which, expelled from a cloud,
immerses in an eternal ocean.

Only what could never be
because we only dreamt,
but not experienced it,
thought of,
but not done,
only rejected,
but not paid as a price owed for our choice,
only that is lost:
nothing remains.

The right moment is ruled over by a god
who appears as a young man
with a curl on his forehead
and a bald head behind.
We may clasp him by the forelock,
but if we reach behind we will grasp nothing."

The young man asked:
"What must I do
that I can still make of myself
what you have been?"
The aged man said:
"Be!"

Applied freedom

The other resurrection from the dead

The resurrection from the dead is the deepest movement of the sprit that we can experience.

Which resurrection from the dead? Is it the resurrection from our own death? In a certain way, yes. But not the resurrection from our death after this life, for we are still alive.

The question is: Are we really alive, or do we live with the dead to a large extent, do we go to them and bring them to us, so that they live on in us, even though they departed a long time ago?

The question is: How do we rise from these dead? How do we return from their death, back into our life?

We let a movement of the spirit take hold of us. This movement is a movement of life, a movement of life, ever new in every moment, now.

What happens to the dead from whom we rise in this movement? They rise from us.

Who is in the way of their resurrection? It is we, we who believe we are alive, even though we dwell among the dead. We who want them to rise back to our life.

Where do they rise then? Instead of rising into their life, they rise into our death, like us, when we draw them to us, into their death.

Looking at it superficially, life and death are mixed up here and turned on their heads. But only for as long as we form images about the movements of the spirit with which we block the experiences that our spirit and our love are capable of accessing. It is a different matter when we dare surrender to the movements of the spirit to the ultimate depth.

The question is: Did we fully wake up to this life through our birth, or did we perhaps wake up to a past life, and to the dead of another life?

Fully awoken to this life, we experience ourselves taken along into a movement that goes on, because this movement calls it into life every moment anew, into the next new life. It takes us along into a movement of life, away from all that was before, away from all the dead, freed from all past, to be purely accomplished.

Accomplished towards what? Even away from this new, in a movement of which it is said, translated into words: "See, I make everything new."

What about the dead then? Are they where we are still looking for them, where we still want to find them? Or have they been taken into the same movement already, a long time ago? Have they woken up to it, so that if we look for them, we stand before empty graves?

The full life has also been elsewhere for them long since, new in every moment, beyond our imaginations, present in a new way, empty of everything from the past. It is there differently, dissolved, uplifted, transcended, arisen. It is there in the light, shining like eternal rising and beginning, forever different, forever new.

So where do we live? Where does all of life live? In a movement of the spirit, eternally present.

About the heaven that makes us ill and the earth that heals us

Heaven and earth

What will be said here about heaven describes what can lead to severe illness or accidents and suicide in the community of fate, containing family and kinship. What will be said about the earth will describe what can still turn such fates around sometimes.

Severe illnesses or accidents and suicide in the family and kinship are brought on by thoughts and actions that join up with images of heaven. Connected to this are images of proxy suffering and proxy penance, of meeting again after death and of personal immortality. These images conjure up magical thinking and wishing and acting, so that the ill or the dying person is believed to be able to redeem the suffering of others through voluntarily taking on their suffering, even if it comes to them in a fated way.

The community of fate

The following people belong to this fated community in which this thinking has its sinister effect: the siblings, the parents and their siblings, the grandparents, sometimes one or the other of the great-grandparents, and all those who made room for one of these.

Among those who made room for others are former marriage partners of parents and grandparents or other serious partners of parents or grandparents, such as former fiancées, and all those whose departure or misfortune opened up access to this group for others or brought them some other kind of advantage.

Family loyalty and its consequences

All the members of this community of fate are inexorably bound together through a deep loyalty. The fateful effects of their loyalty are strongest when they spring from the love of a child toward his/her parents, or when it is loyalty between siblings, or between husband and wife. But a special loyalty is also felt by those who gained an advantage through those who had to leave. In this way, a husband's second wife often demonstrates an unconscious loyalty to his first wife, or the children of a second marriage may be secretly loyal toward the children of their mother or father's first marriage. The loyalty of parents to their children is less strong than that of children toward their parents. We also observe powerful and unexpected loyalties between perpetrators and their victims and between veterans of war and their fallen comrades.

Similarity and balance

This loyalty results in the weaker members of the group wanting to hold onto the stronger ones to prevent them from leaving or dying, or, if they have already gone, in wanting to follow them.

It also results in those who have an advantage sharing the fate of those with a disadvantage, and sharing responsibility for the health, happiness, innocence, and life of the less fortunate members of their family; children, for example, may act this way toward their ill parents or siblings, or innocent children may try to bear their parent's guilt.

Thus those with an advantage often risk – and lose – their health, innocence, and life, for the health, innocence, and life of others, following the magical hope that by renouncing their own happiness and their own lives they may save the lives and happiness of others.

This loyalty among the members of the family and extended family manifests as a need for systemic balance between the benefits enjoyed by one member and the disadvantages suffered by another. It is this systemic urge for balance that leads one member of the group to court misfortune when another is suffering, or that tempts one person into illness or misfortune when another is ill or guilty, or that makes someone long for death when another member of the system dies.

Thus, within this confined fellowship of fate, loyalty and the need for balance and compensation assures that one member participates in the guilt and illness and fate and death of others; it leads to attempts to bring about someone's well-being through one's own misfortune, someone else's health through one's own illness, someone else's guilt through one's own innocence, or someone else's innocence through one's own guilt, and someone else's life through one's own death.

The illness follows the soul

Since the systemic need for balance and compensation courts illness and death, illness follows the soul, out of a heartfelt desire to belong to our fellowship of fate. Thus, in addition to medical help in the more usual sense, psychological help and care are also necessary to bring about healing. But whereas doctors actively do all they can to cure their patients' illnesses, psychotherapists aware of the systemic dimension of illness are more restrained since they understand that they are working with forces of love and belonging with which it would be presumptuous to compete. Their work is limited to helping their clients and patients align and harmonize with these forces, as an ally rather than as their rival. Here is an example:

"Better me than you"

During a group hypnotherapy session, a woman suffering from multiple sclerosis saw herself kneeling by the bed of her paralyzed mother and deciding in her heart: "Better me than you, Mummy dear. I will suffer in your place." Everyone in the group was moved by the child's love, but one participant, ignoring the depth and intensity of this love, implored the therapist, "You've got to get her out of that!"

But how can we presume to insult the child's love by intervening in that way? Surely trying to get her to renounce her childhood promise can only increase her suffering, rather than alleviate it, forcing her to hide her love and cling all the more secretly to her determination to save her mother though her own suffering.

What a doctor or psychotherapist can do – and what he or she must be careful to avoid – may become clear with another example. A young woman, also suffering from multiple sclerosis, set up a family constellation with the mother on the right of the father. Opposite them stood the patient herself; on her left her younger brother, who died of heart failure at the age of 14; and to his left, the youngest child, another brother.

Following the representatives' reports, the psychotherapist had the dead brother's representative leave the room, which reflected the reality of his death. When he had left the room, the face of the client's representative immediately brightened up, and it was obvious that her mother was also feeling much more comfortable. Because he had observed that the representatives of both father and the younger brother felt an urge to leave, the psychotherapist had them leave the room as well. When all the men had left the room (signifying that they had died), the mother straightened up with a relieved expression on her face, and it became clear to everyone present that she was the one who was under systemic pressure to die – for whatever reason – and that she was touched and relieved that the men in her family were ready to die in her place.

To make the underlying dynamic clearer, the psychotherapist called the men back and had the mother leave the room. Immediately, all the other representatives felt liberated from the systemic pressure to take the mother's fate upon themselves, and they all felt much better.

To test the possibility that the daughter's multiple sclerosis was systemically connected with the mother's hidden belief that she should die, the therapist called the mother back into the room, placed her to the left of her husband, and placed the daughter next to her mother.

He asked the daughter to look straight into her mother's eyes and say to her with love: "Mother, I will do it for you!" As she said the words, her face grew radiant, and the systemic meaning and objective of her illness became clear to everyone.

So what is the doctor or the psychotherapist allowed to do here, and what must be avoided?

The knowing love

Often all a psychotherapist can do is to bring the child's love to light and to trust the dynamic of love itself to find what is truly needed. For no matter what the child took upon himself or herself, it was done in good conscience and with the conviction that it was the right and noble thing to do. When, however, this love comes to light through the help of an understanding psychotherapist, it also becomes clear to the child that blind love can never achieve its objective.

Children cherish the magical hope that, through sacrifice, they may heal their loved ones, protect them from harm, atone for their guilt and snatch them from the jaws of death. But as adults, when their blind love is brought to light, and also their childlike hopes and desires, they may realize that their blind love and sacrifice inevitably must fail to overcome a loved one's illness, suffering and death.

When the objectives of a child's love and the means used to achieve them are brought to light, they lose their magical power because they are rooted in magical beliefs that cannot survive in the adult world. The love, however, endures. More discriminating when combined with reason, the very same love that once caused illness, now seeks a different, enlightened solution, and, if it is still possible, to fulfill the true goals of love, making illness unnecessary. The doctor and psychotherapist may show the direction, but the child-soul must rest assured that they respect his or her love, and that they only work to help the love achieve its goals in a better way.

"I shall disappear instead of you"

One of the most common magical beliefs accompanying life-threatening disease is a child's decision: "I will go instead of you."

In the case of anorexia, the child's soul often decides: "I will go instead of you, Daddy dear," and in the preceding example of multiple sclerosis, the child's decision was: "I will go instead of you, Mummy dear." Similar dynamics are at work in tuberculosis.

These dynamics also are often found operating behind suicide and fatal accidents.

"Even if you go, I'll stay"

What is the helpful and healing solution when these dynamics come to light? The solution emerges when you stand face to face with the beloved person, and with all the power and conviction of love, speak the sentences of blind love, "I will go instead of you." Sometimes, you need to repeat the sentences a few times until you recognize the loved one as an individual person and, notwithstanding the depth of love, as separate and apart. If this doesn't happen, the symbiosis and identification will remain, but there is an unmistakable sweetness and innocence, an atmospheric gentleness and simplicity when the sentences are spoken from the depth of the child's soul.

A person who succeeds in saying the words with the whole force and conviction of love, affirms the child's love, but affirms it in a different context, standing as an adult face to face with the beloved person. This combination of affirmation of the child's love and adult contact allows the child-soul to realize that the other loves as well, both are adults, lover and beloved to one another. This knowing love draws a line between them, and thus between their individual destinies. It makes possible the realization that the other gains nothing from my sacrifice, on the contrary, my efforts to intervene in favor of the beloved person are more likely to burden than to help.

Raising love from blind love to knowing love challenges our magical beliefs and changes the sentences that describe the dynamics of love, "Father dear, Mother dear, my dear brother, my dear sister – or whoever it may be – even if you go, I will stay." Some people add: "Mother dear, Father dear, bless me when I stay, and please wish me well even if you go."

Let me illustrate this by an example. A woman's father had two handicapped brothers, one of them deaf and the other psychotic. He was systemically pulled to his brothers and to their fate, and out of loyalty to them, he could not bear to see their suffering alongside his own well-being. His daughter unconsciously recognized his danger and leaped into the breach. When she set up her family constellation, her representative rushed over to her father's brothers and embraced them as if she were saying in her heart: "Father dear, I will leave so that you can stay." The client had anorexia.

What is the solution here? The daughter must first look at her father's brothers as individuals and then say to them in her heart: "Please love my father if he stays with us, and love me if I stay with my father."

"I will follow you"

Another, earlier sentence lies behind the parents' desire to leave or to die, which the child tries to prevent with the words: "Better me than you." It is a sentence that the parents may want to say to their own ill or dead parents or siblings: "I will follow you," or, more precisely: "I will follow you into your illness," or: "I will follow you into death."

Thus, in the family, the first sentence to take its effect is: "I will follow you." These are the words of a child. And, when these children grow up, their own children prevent them from implementing the words by saying: "Better me than you."

"I will go on living for a little while"

Whenever the dynamic "I will follow you" is operating in the background of fatal illness and accidents or suicide, the helpful and healing solution is, first of all, to bring the dynamic to light by allowing the child to speak the words aloud to the beloved person with all the power and conviction of the child's love. Usually, the words that name the dynamic are some variation of the sentence, "Father dear, Mother dear, dear brother, dear sister – or whomever it may be – I will follow you, even into death."

Here, too, it is important that the words be repeated as often as it takes for the patient to recognize and perceive the loved ones as individual, separate beings. Publicly naming this dynamic allows the child to realize that love cannot eliminate the separation between the living and the dead, and that we all must recognize and accept these limits. As the child's blind love develops into knowing love, it is easier for the child to see that it is easier for the loved ones to fulfill their own destiny when no one interferes, especially not their own children.

Many people in constellations have found another sentence to be very freeing, "Father dear, Mother dear, dear brother, dear sister – or whoever it may be – you are dead. I will go on living for a little while, and then I, too, will die." Or: "I will live my life fully, as long as it lasts, and then I, too, will die."

When children see that one of the parents is drawn to follow someone from their family of origin into illness and death, they can free themselves when they can authentically say, "Father dear, Mother dear, even if you go, I stay," or "Even if you go, I honor you as my father, and I honor you as my mother." Or, if one of the parents has committed suicide: "I respect your decision and bow to your fate, and I honor you as my father, and I honor you as my mother."

Beliefs that cause illness

The two sentences, "Better me than you" and "I will follow you," are secretly spoken by entangled children with utterly innocent conviction. At the same time, they correspond to the Christian message and the Christian example, for instance, to Christ's words in the Gospel of St. John, "Greater love hath no man than this, that a man lay down his life for his friends," and also to the Christian tradition that true believers should be willing to follow him on the way of the cross and into death.

The Christian teaching of redemption through suffering and death and the example of Christian saints and heroes confirm children's magical hope and magical belief that they can take on illness and suffering and death in someone else's place. By paying in the currency of suffering, they hope to redeem others from their suffering, and to rescue them from death by dying in their place. And they also hope that if redemption is no longer possible on this earth, they will be reunited with the departed loved ones if they, like them, lose their life and (so they believe) find it again through death.

The love that heals

In such entanglements, healing and redemption are beyond mere medical and therapeutic measures. They require a religious process. They require a change of heart towards something greater that goes beyond magical and wishful thinking and strips it of its powers.

This greater would be – in opposition to the treacherous promises of heaven – the earth. Saying yes to the earth means saying yes to her fullness and also to life's beginning and end.

Sometimes, it is possible for a doctor or helper to pave the way for such a change of heart and support it, but it is not in the doctor or helper's power to achieve it. It does not follow a method of cause and effect.

Illness as atonement

The need to atone for guilt is another of the systemic forces that leads to illness, accidents, suicide and premature death.

In many cultures, atonement is seen as being something valuable and good, but if we look at it systemically, we see that it is a cruel distortion, which only perpetuates suffering. Events that were unavoidable and determined by fate are sometimes treated as if they carried a personal guilt and required atonement. For example, a parent may become ill or despondent following a miscarriage or the illness, or early death of a child. In such cases, it is more helpful for the parent to look at the deceased child with love, to face the grief the death entails, and to allow the past to be past.

Similarly, people may become ill or harm themselves following events that bring benefit or even life to one person while harming another. For instance, when a mother dies in childbirth, her child often has difficulty fully claiming success in life, as if his or her failure could atone for the mother's sacrifice.

There are other situations in which someone is genuinely responsible for causing harm, for example, when someone, without a pressing need, aborts a child or gives it away, or ruthlessly inflicts wrong on someone else. Atonement for personal guilt frequently takes place on a subconscious level and in direct opposition to the mother's protestations of innocence or justification of her actions.

In these situations too, the person comes under systemic pressure to atone for the guilt, whether real or imagined, by compensating for the suffering of others through his or her own suffering. Or, as we have seen in many examples, one of the children takes on the burden. But when our guilt is real, what helps is doing good, not adding to suffering by suffering ourselves.

Such distorted practices, disastrous as they are for all involved, of attempting compensation through atonement, is actually promoted by religious teaching, by the belief in redemption through suffering and dying and the belief in cleansing of sin and guilt through self-inflicted punishment and physical suffering and pain.

Compensation through atonement is suffering doubled

Atonement satisfies our blind need for compensation and balance. But when this compensation is sought through illness, accidents and death, what is really achieved? Instead of one injured person, there are two, and one death is followed by a second. Worse still, atonement doubles the damage done to the victim, because the victim's suffering becomes the cause of more suffering, and his or her own death results in someone else's dying.

Atonement is illusory, as if one's own suffering or death could really bring about someone else's healing or redemption.

The wish to atone for someone else's guilt entails the wish to pay for like with like. Suffering takes the place of constructive action, death the place of life, and atonement the place of guilt.

A child whose mother dies when giving birth feels guilty because the mother paid for the child's life with her death. If this child tries to atone for her death by suffering or suicide, then the disaster becomes even greater for the mother – she loses her own life and her child dies. Then, the life she gave her child is not honored, and her love is not recognized and appreciated. Her death will have been in vain and, worse still, it will have brought suffering instead of happiness, and instead of one death there are two.

If we want to help a child in this situation, we must look clearly at what atonement really achieves, we must penetrate its illusion and distortion, and we must remember that in addition to the desire for systemic balance through atonement, the child also has the wish: "Better me than you" and "I will follow you." We can abandon our ill-fated longing for atonement only if we leave behind the words: "Better me than you" and "I will follow you."

Balance through taking and reconciling actions

What, then, is the appropriate solution for both the child and the mother? The child must say: "Mother dear, the price you paid for my life is not in vain: I will make something of my life, in memory of you and in your honor."

This means that the child must act constructively instead of suffering, achieve good instead of failing, and live fully instead of dying.

In so doing the child becomes much more deeply united with the mother than by following her into suffering and death.

Remaining symbiotically connected with the mother the child is connected in a numb and blind way, but by accepting and living life fully, the child embraces the mother in his or her heart, and strength and grace flow from Mother to the child.

Unlike compensation through atonement, which increases suffering and death, this compensation leads to happiness and health. Compensation through atonement is cheap, harmful, and grasping and fails to achieve reconciliation; compensation through positive action is costly and bestows blessings. Then, both the mother and the child become reconciled to their fate, for the mother participates in the life and achievements of her child.

This would be the difference between magical balance and a balance that is in accord with the earth. It heeds the insight that our life is unique, that, in its vanishing, it makes room for what is coming, and even though it may be gone, it still nourishes what is now.

Penance as a substitute for relationship

Through atonement we avoid facing the relationship. Through atonement we deal with our guilt as if it were a thing with which we pay for damage. But what can such penance achieve when I have done a person injustice, when I caused this person misfortune, and harmed this person in body and soul, caused irreparable damage to this person's life? The idea that I can unburden myself through penance, by hurting myself, is only possible if I do not look at the other. If I turn to the other, I must acknowledge that what I really want is to do away with something that must remain.

This also needs to be heeded in guilt for which we are personally responsible. Often a mother seeks to do penance for an abortion or a loss of a child in some other way with a terminal illness or by giving up the relationship to the child's father and renouncing any future relationship.

The penance for a personal guilt usually occurs subconsciously, in spite of her denial or declaration.

Sometimes with mothers, apart from the need for penance there is also the wish to follow the dead child, just as a child wants to follow a dead mother. But even a child who lost his or her life through the mother, we may assume, will say: "Rather me than you." When the mother becomes ill and dies as penance, the child's death out of love for the mother was in vain.

In case of a personal guilt the solution is also to replace penance with reconciling action. This happens through relating to the person whom I treated unjustly, or on whom I imposed terrible things. For instance, a mother who aborted a child, or disowned or abandoned the child, looks into the child's eyes and then says: "I am sorry" and "I give you a place in my heart" and "I will make up for it the best I still can" and "You shall have your share in the good that I achieve in memory of you and with you before me."

Then the guilt would not be in vain, for the good that the mother achieves in memory of this child and with a view to this child, happens with the child and through the child. The child participates in it and still remains connected with the mother and with what she is doing for some time.

Guilt comes to an end on earth

There is something else to keep in mind about guilt. It will pass and it must be allowed to be over. Only in the face of heaven is there an eternal guilt. On earth it is transient. Like everything on earth it is over after some time.

Illness as attempt to atone for someone else

Guilt and penance are frequently taken on by others in the family. Concerning guilt and penance a child or a partner also says: "Rather me than you." They take on what others refuse to carry as their own guilt and the consequences.

In a group a mother shared that she had refused to bring her old mother into her home to look after her, instead, she put her into a nursing home. In the same week her daughter became anorexic. She only dressed in black and went to a nursing home twice a week to care for old people. Nobody, not even the daughter, understood the connections.

Illness as a result of refusing to honor one's parents

Another attitude leading to severe illness is the refusal of children to take their parents with love and to honor them as parents. Such children rise above the earth, because they deem themselves as better or chosen, in the face of heaven or some other higher authority. Cancer patients sometimes would rather die than bow to their mother or their father.

To honor one's parents is to honor the earth

Those believing in heaven also believe that with the help of heaven they can rise above the earth and above their parents. Honoring the parents is honoring the earth. Honoring the parents means taking them and loving them as they are, taking them and loving them with life and death, with health and illness, with beginning and end. This is the real religious attitude at one time called surrender and devotion. We experience it as utter relinquishing, taking everything and giving everything – with love.

Faces of love

We begin with love from deep down below, with conception in our mother's womb. At one with her, we feel her love. We feel how she loves us, when she strokes her belly; we hear her voice, when she lovingly talks to us, or about us, to others.

As we are one with her, we feel it directly when she expresses her love to others, to our father for instance. At the same time we also feel her other feelings, her fears and worries for instance. We feel it when she feels guilty and when she is upset with others. We resonate with her through thick and thin.

We also respond to her, with our movements, for instance. Thus begins an early interplay. Through her this is also an interplay with the surroundings that await us after our birth.

So from very early on we experience an essential secret of love. Love goes back and forth. More precisely, it comes to us and then it returns to where the love came from.

It's the same with life. At first it comes and then it responds. Our life is embedded in a movement of coming from and going to, in a very basic way, with its complete existence. In this sense life is love.

After our birth we must bridge a gap with our life and our love. The love comes from someone and it goes to someone, in the first instance to our mother.

This love is close body contact, especially when the mother takes the child to her breast. Mother and child look tenderly at each other.

This love flows back and forth in several ways, first of all as nourishment. The child still lives off the mother. With the mother's milk the child takes the mother in also, and the child grows through her substance.

How does the child respond to this love? It takes it, suckling at its mother's breast and then falling asleep in deep contentment.

At the same time the child has body contact with the mother in many other ways. The child is dressed, changed, put to bed, held, stroked. Other people join in, above all the father, and then the grandparents, the older siblings, the aunties and uncles.

In this way the child feels embedded in the family and deeply connected with it. The child responds to their love by looking at them, and soon there is also a smile.

The child cries when he or she needs something, and straight away someone comes to the rescue, calming and helping.

Love is tender exchange with an increasing number of people. The child experiences this love, above all, as taking. The child receives what he or she needs, and responds to this love by seeking closeness with the others and cuddling up to them. More and more love also comes forth from the child, and others respond to it.

Beyond the people, this love also begins to venture out into the near surroundings. First of all to the animals, to a cat or a dog or a bird. On a farm it goes to many other animals, to a horse for instance, especially a pony, or a goat, a sheep, a rabbit, a chick. Here, too, the love goes to and fro and becomes rich this way.

The child learns to take care of animals, learns to observe them, and learns to give them food and to stroke them. The child experiences the animals' love when they want to make physical contact with the child, for instance, by jumping up and licking the child.

The child continually explores his or her surroundings. Perhaps he or she observes a frog, even imitates it, catches a maybug and lets its fly away again. In this exchange with the surroundings he or she becomes one with it.

But after a while the child always returns to the mother and father. The child comes home again.

Above all, in this early time the child learns to play with other children, in a constant to and fro, including arguments and separation, and coming back together again.

Early childhood, roughly up to the fifth year, is a rich time with the basic experiences of love in love's rich back and forth, including the tests that accompany it.

The question is: How much of this remains in our adult life? How much of this intense to and fro of love remains alive in us? Can we bring these experiences back to life? Was there a break? What has pushed these early experiences into the background and covered them up?

It was practically always an early separation, especially from the mother, whatever the circumstances were that could not be changed. An extended illness of the mother or even her early death are examples of this interruption. Or perhaps the child had to go elsewhere for a long time, or perhaps he or she was even given away. Then the originally safe world of love broke down for the child, the to and fro of love – love's trustworthy to and fro – ended to a large extent.

Like any other trauma, this trauma is also resolved when the movements that were suddenly interrupted and no longer possible are taken up again and brought to their destination.

This is an inner process. It succeeds through a change in our attention. Instead of looking at the images we saved of this separation, and the feelings that come along with them, we reanimate the other, earlier images and connected to them, the feelings of a carefree bliss.

Then inside us, as the child from that time, we walk the path to our mother once more, as it was then. We go back to the original love, to the original taking and giving, to the original bliss.

From this restored perspective, we can even look differently at the later years of our childhood that were burdened by those images of separation.

How many people came towards us in those years, being helpful and kind? How did we respond to their love with ours? How rich in love was even this time? How rich is it still now for us, when we bring it back into our memory and into our heart?

The same goes for our youth, where we tried to become more and more independent, with occasional separation from our family, then even for longer periods, now already with clear goals before us, of what we wanted to do later in life. Where is this development heading, first as a practice run and then more seriously? All the love that we were allowed to experience until then, including the trials, were aiming towards the love with a partner for life.

Taking and giving are reaching new dimensions here. I will not go into this dimension here, for its faces look into the far distance, creatively far. I am looking into this direction in devotion, without fathoming it.

There, in this distance an ultimate love is shining. In accord with this love, we breathe with it, with this love that thought our life, and that called us into this life with love. Only in this love do we find fulfillment and accomplishment. In a shared rhythm with this love, our life and our love pulsates, even beyond this life.

This love loves everything as it is, the small and the big, the beginning and the end. It loves us the same as everything else. We respond to it by being there, lovingly there, there with everything else, back home with it, at one with everything that is there with us.

Thoughts of peace

Peace to the dead

Most of the dead are at peace, and any concerns about them and any thoughts of them disturb their peace. They are beyond our world.

I have an image of life. Life is an interlude between what was before and what will be afterwards. Therefore the unborn and the accomplished are equally taken care of. If someone wants to get in touch with them, for instance because he or she wants to put something in order with them because he or she feels guilty towards them, the dead do not understand it.

But we also experience that some of the dead still have their effect on the present. They are not at peace yet. Sometimes they attach themselves to the living and draw them into death. These dead need help. It seems these dead do not realize that they are dead. They are still seeking nourishment from the living and suck them dry. To engage with them and give in to them is dangerous.

How can we escape them? We escape them in our pure existence. In their presence, we dissolve as it were, into pure relating, so that nothing is left of us that they could attach themselves to. In this pure relating one is fully permeable, one looks away from them towards a mysterious dark, and then remains recollected in its presence. This has the effect that the dead are also turning there, away from the living. We allow them to dissolve there, into something that Richard Wagner calls: Blissful primordial forgetting.

Where does peace begin? Where memory ends. The deepest longing in everything is the entering of this forgetting.

I went out on a limb here. But what I am speaking of here is only to get a sense of which movements are possible and what effects they have in our soul and in the souls of others.

What is the worst for the dead? Remembering them. Not in the beginning, memory is still alive then. But dying is apparently a process of gradual release of oneself. This process, the process of releasing, should not be opposed. For instance through memory.

The biography of a deceased interferes in this process. Every accusation, every complaint, every extended grief, interferes in this process.

A little while ago I opened a book to read something about the crusades. Suddenly I became aware that if I read on, I would get in the way of the peace between the perpetrators and the victims. Then I closed the book.

Forgetting is an aspect of the highest love.

Who among the dead fare best? Which ones have completed their dying and have eternal peace? Those whom we allow to be forgotten.

We can also imagine how it would be for us if we die and are remembered, or if we die and are forgotten. Where is the accomplishment?

After some time all the dead must be given the right to be forgotten.

Sometimes there is still something in the way. They expect of us that we respect them, that we perhaps still thank them and still grieve for them. Only then are they free from us and we from them.

Blessing and curse

The blessing comes from above and flows down. It comes to us from someone who is higher than we are. Those who bless us are above all our parents. When parents bless their children, they are most deeply connected with the flow of life. The parents' blessing accompanies the life they have passed on to their children. As life does, the blessing also reaches far beyond the parents. As life, the blessing is a passing on of something sacred that we received ourselves earlier on.

The blessing is a yes to life. It guards life; it adds to life, it walks with life. At the same time it releases the blessed children into their own life, into their fullness. The blessing and the fullness flow through the children onto others, to their partners for instance, to their own children, to friends. And they flow over into their actions, so that they may support and guard life in an all-embracing way.

Thus the parents bless their children when they leave. They themselves remain behind. From now on the children stand on their own two feet. And also when the parents say farewell to their children, when they die for instance, they bless their children and grandchildren. In this blessing they remain connected to them.

So therefore only those who are blessed themselves and in harmony with something greater can and may bless others. They only pass on what has reached them and what they have opened up to themselves. The act of blessing is humble. Only where it is humble can it unfold the gift of bestowing blessings.

The opposite of blessing, its shadow as it were, is the curse. Through the curse ill-will is sent toward another person. The curse is meant to harm another's life, even destroy it. Similar to the blessing that reaches beyond an individual to the descendants, the curse is often not only meant to hurt one person, but also the children of that person.

People with ill wishes for someone else and for their children have often suffered injustice or believe that injustice was done to them. If someone has good cause to be angry, reconciliation must happen. One must acknowledge the injustice and ask the other to accept the regret and be friendly again. This succeeds more easily when the injured person is asked to also look kindly on the children of the offending person, wishing them well. In other words, to bless them.

In ourselves we sense sometimes that we have ill wishes towards others and that we refuse to really wish them well. This can be seen in small things at times, for instance if we object to something that would further the other person or makes them happy. Through our objection we tie the person to us, instead of letting them go to lead their own life and to be in their own fullness.

How can we face this? We can practice being a blessing. For instance, after meeting with people or at the end of the day, we can ask: "Have I been a blessing here today?" Then in blessing we experience ourselves more and more blessed from day to day.

Often people have ill wishes towards others, without even knowing them. Then suddenly someone feels exposed to someone's ill will, against which he or she has no defense. Such people cannot undo this through actions of their own, for they may not even know the person who wishes them harm. How can individuals protect themselves in their soul so that this ill will does not eat up their lives, diminish their lives, perhaps making them ill and draining their will to live? They turn to the source of life, open to its fullness and its power, and let these flow through them, with such strength that they also reach the others who want to limit their life and stem the flow of goodness. Thus they also meet a curse with blessings.

Love also for the perpetrators

Perpetrators can soften once they are loved. The campaigns that are sometimes run in Germany and Austria, with the motto: "This must never happen again," often have an opposite effect. Whilst the perpetrators do not have a place in our midst and in our hearts as well, the bad, their bad, still has power. The more they are rejected, the more strength they gain.

When they are accepted by us, they can be humans like us again. Only then can they grieve – and also face the consequences, not before.

Something else we need to consider here. Under the influence of our conscience we distinguish between good and bad. The good ones, they're ours, the bad ones belong to the others. But the others think the same: We are the good ones; the others are the bad ones.

It is also disastrous here, when, looking at such terrible events as the Holocaust and the Second World War and all the crimes that happened then, we attribute all this to the responsibility of individuals. We have the idea that if only we educate our children differently, then this will never happen again. The overcoming of the past is seen as the responsibility and within the strength of individuals, as if they had the power for this.

In this we completely delude ourselves about the incredible impact of historic events that capture whole nations and force them into something that is largely inescapable for most individuals. For the Germans and the Austrians this was the case. No one could have stopped it.

It was also inescapable for the Jewish people. Nobody could have prevented or halted it. All were at the mercy of a vastly greater power.

As long as we do not look at this greater power and acknowledge it in its horror, as long as we do not bow and submit to it, there is no solution. Therefore in the end the solution is a religious achievement and consummation.

The key to reconciliation between perpetrators and victims is ultimately in the hands of the victims. The perpetrators are powerless until a movement comes from the victims that also allows the perpetrators to move. The perpetrators cannot do this on their own accord.

We also need to keep something else in mind: The dead victims have no peace until they have given the dead perpetrators a place by their side. This reconciliation proceeds among the dead, not among the living. The living cannot intervene here.

When we as survivors and offspring acknowledge that we must not meddle in this, that we must let this process among the dead take its course, we can distance ourselves more easily from this past.

As long as we take sides for one lot against the other, we prevent reconciliation. What are we doing when at official memorials we think of the victims of the last war, and what do we need to do when people speak about it. We are expected to take sides against the bad and for the victims. What is the result? Perpetrators and victims cannot come together, because we step between them through our judgment and our way of remembering.

The healing movement towards peace in our soul would be agreeing to both, agreeing to their fate, as it was, be it as perpetrator, be it as victim. Both at once. Then we also reconcile the murderous dimension in ourselves, our own murderous impulse, and the suffering at the hands of others, where we experience ourselves as victims. Both at once. Only when these two sides can come together have we become whole as human beings.

The end of revenge

I will do a little exercise with you now. We close our eyes and recollect ourselves in our center. We go beyond your body, into the realm of the dead, and we look at the dead of our own family.

Then we look beyond them, at the millions of dead people who perished, who were murdered, who died of starvation and torture. They are all lying there. And side by side with them, also lying on the ground, are the perpetrators – those who killed them, maltreated and tortured them, made them starve to death.

There are also the dead from the war. So many. The dead soldiers and the dead civilians. The many who were murdered, left to starve, tortured. All are dead. The soldiers from both sides are also lying there, enemies to each other. All dead. All the same. None better. None worse. All dead. A huge army of the dead from all sides.

And far beyond the horizon a white light is shining, still below the horizon. One only sees its glow. The dead get up, turn to the light and bow deeply, the dead victims and the dead perpetrators. And we bow with them. All bow in devotion before this light that remains partly hidden.

While the dead remain in this devotion, we get up, walking backwards, and we leave the dead to themselves, the victims and the perpetrators. We withdraw further and further, until we lose sight of them. Then we turn around, we come back into life and we look to the future.

Here all revenge comes to an end.

The spirit and the spiritual

Sometimes we use the word spirit and behave as if it were at our disposal. Sometimes in our daily living and working we discover something, a law or an order for instance. Then we think we have discovered something special. And it's true, in a certain, transient way.

But the spirit does not operate according to our discoveries. We cannot refer to the spirit or the spiritual when we apply what we discovered, as if it were now the truth or the final state. When evolution ends, life ends. When changes no longer happen, life does not go on. When the flow of new insights ends, we atrophy.

So let us remain open for the spiritual, leaving the past behind us. Otherwise the old will disturb the new. Therefore an ongoing openness for surprises is necessary.

Is the former wrong then? Is the first step on a path wrong, because it does not immediately lead to the destination? The first step is as important as the last one. All have their place. But the best of all is always the next step.

The last place

When we look at our ancestors and the many generations through which life has reached us, we stand at the most recent and also the last place. The last place is the place where everything flows together. The whole fullness that has gathered over the many generations reaches us because we are down on the ground and remain there. The last place is therefore a place of fullness.

Some think they must still do something for their ancestors; perhaps something has to be put in order for them. Then they behave as if our ancestors needed something from us. They want to turn back the stream of life, so that it flows from below to above.

Some want to avenge their ancestors, want to return their rights to them and to expiate an injustice done to them, as if they were lacking something. Then we rise above them and above their fate, and we lose something of our fate and our life. Instead of taking our life and holding it firmly, we sacrifice it to our dead. This is of course a strange idea.

Our ancestors are complete. It is only we who still have our completion ahead of us. Therefore it is important that we who are in the last place see everything that was before us as complete and over.

Some also think that they have taken on a legacy from their forebears, for instance to carry on what they inherited. Then we behave as if there wasn't just our life that we received from them, but also something else to which we must sacrifice a part of our life. With this, we refuse to take our life fully in its entirety.

So if we only look at our ancestors as those through whom life poured forth to us, if we look only to this life and forget everything else, we suddenly find ourselves in the last place, with nothing left that could come between our life and us. There, like all other people, being in the last place we also have the first place.

The last place is the place of the spirit. Veering away from the spirit, we leave the last place, and then we are deserted by spirit, abandoned until we perhaps come to our senses again through the help of the spirit.

Ecumenicalism

Reconciled

At the end of this book the question comes up: What about ecumenicalism? How is the reconciliation among the different Christian churches going? Does ecumenicalism have a future? What would need to happen for it to succeed?

The Christian churches would have to leave a range of beliefs behind, such as the belief in the resurrection from the dead, and the belief in his Second Coming. Connected to that, also the belief in the physical resurrection of all the dead and the Last Judgment with its separation of the damned and the chosen for eternity. But especially the image of god that makes Christians cringe with constant fear that they might also be among the damned, which means they have to spend a big part of their life trying to escape this threat.

What are the churches doing to their adherents when they preach this belief and this fear of god, thus keeping them in constant fear and terror?

Compared to this fear, how trivial are many ecumenical attempts to bring the churches closer together, for instance in a shared formulation of the justification doctrine.

The question is: What is really expected and demanded from the Christian churches?

What the Christians are jointly demanding is the farewell from that god to whom even Jesus fell prey. They demand a farewell to the god who can be insulted and who demands from all human beings lifelong caution and penance, so that they escape eternal damnation.

So the churches demand the turning away from an image of god that cannot be imagined more absurdly, and together with this image of god, also the farewell to heaven and the returning to the earth as it is.

This image is an image of the future. The question comes up: Can the churches face these images? How do they conduct themselves towards their adherents if they continue to declare this god that must be feared, and the resurrected and returning Jesus who must also be feared? How can they uphold the love for Jesus and Jesus' love?

Humility

Humility remains on the ground. Because it stays on the ground it is most completely in unison with yonder creative power that knows no distinctions because it is at one with everything at its very origin. How else could anything exist if it were not willed and held by this power? All oppositions, including all those things we want to be different, our mistakes and their consequences, for example – are wanted by it. Every arising and vanishing, everything old and new, all are wanted. Humility fits in with everything that may come; however it comes, with everything it costs us.

Therefore humility moves on with time as it comes. It goes with the time as it was, without glorifying the past or rejecting it, for the past, whatever it was, goes with the future. It has its effect because it was as it was and it enforces the new, as it must come. Therefore the new knows no regret about the old, nor the wish to have a past that is different from how it was, regardless of the far-reaching consequences it had for us and the world.

On the other hand, because of its lack of pride and self-aggrandizement, humility is willing to serve bravely, whatever the new times may demand from the humble. Courageously remaining on the ground, without rising above the former state, humility gives no cause to those who might want to rise above it. The humble only need to go down a bit further, there where the earth will receive them as one with her.

Another aspect of humble yet courageous thinking and acting is the option of correcting a false move, without falling into an abyss. Only from a height can we fall far.

This also applies to the religions and the churches. The closer they remain to the earth, the closer they remain to life and love.

What happens to them when they have gone too far, reaching dizzying heights? How can they come back down safely?

Here, too, they come back down to the ground step by step, until they arrive where they experience themselves carried by the earth. They experience themselves stripped of their myths, as earthly beings, with both feet on the ground that holds us firmly.

What would be the sentence here, the humble, freeing sentence that holds true for all?

Rilke told us:

Earth, you dear one, I will.

Nostalgia

We feel nostalgia when we look back. This is how I feel when I think back about the achievements of the churches, of their music, their tall cathedrals, their works of art, of the many ways of caring and helping with love. These achievements belong to their great and elevating aspects.

On the other hand there is their dogmatism, their persecution, their inquisition that took many forms, their accumulated wealth, their pomp, and, above all, the wars they waged.

Can these two sides balance out? Or does the heavy burden at one end push the light side up even higher for a time?

For many people the churches turned into a refuge, a safe home, a hope in desperate times. Yet even above those in dire need the terrible god swings his scepter.

Am I permitted to look back at the church in this nostalgic way? Do I have to leave all of this behind? Can I take something with me? Is there a cut, a boundary that demands a farewell forever from me? Nostalgic at first, and freeing later on?

Over

Nothing is over; everything still has its effect. The question is: Does it repeat itself and does it deplete itself? Does it collapse, because something new takes its place? Does it collapse under the influence of something outside, like a kingdom collapses through a revolution? Or does it collapse through increased knowledge and understanding and a new orientation? Can it, though collapsing, rise up again, at least for a time? Does it only fade away slowly, like our life, when it's at its end and dragging out, becoming less and less, until it is finally extinguished?

Sometimes what passed and collapsed in this way leaves remarkable ruins behind. We admire them without being moved by them. They remain in the past.

Can the next phase take up their place as if it could endure without passing? Does this also apply to those movements that took the place of the churches, like the national states, or enlightenment or democracy or the human rights movement, or the freedom of conscience? Or can we already see their limits too?

We prepare for their passing also, without rising above them as if they were over already. Do we know how far we can move on with them? Do we remain careful, without presumptuousness? Do we remain on the ground in these matters as well?

Can the time on the ground also be over? Does it also have a gradient towards more? Can we leave everything in the past in this movement, in a way that we gain? Where we gain everything?

I have summed up these movements in three sentences:

There on the ground.

Whole on the ground.

Eternal on the ground.

With this I close this book and breathe a deep sigh of relief. When I began I did not know where it would take me. To begin with, much in this book frightened me because I asked myself whether I demanded too much from myself and from others. Too much was at stake.

I have grown with this book. In the first instance, I imposed too much on myself, sometimes painfully, but in the end freeing.

Now I put the book into your hands and in the hands of the powers that stood and stand behind everything, including the churches.

Voices from afar

Dalai Lama

The renowned spokesman of Buddhism surprised his audience with the statement that in ethical questions one shouldn't necessarily refer to religions. On his facebook page it says:

"All great world religions with their emphasis on love, forgiveness, compassion, patience, tolerance, and forgiveness can support inner values. The reality of our world today is, however, that it is no longer in keeping with the times to base our ethics on religions. For this reason, I arrive more and more at the conviction that the time has come to think about spirituality and ethics completely beyond all religions."

William Commanda

William Commanda, a well respected Elder of the Algonquin people in Canada, was an honourary guest at a workshop I gave in Ottawa. Later I visited him in his house, with some friends.

During our conversation he suddenly said: "In our language there is no word for justice."

I asked him: "Then what happens to a murderer in your nation?"

He said: "The murderer is adopted by the family, of the victim..."

I was speechless.

William Commanda died in 2011 at 98 years old.

Ibn Arabi

In the midst of the Crusades, the Arab thinker, Ibn Arabi (1165–1240), said:

"Oh magnificence! A Garden amidst flames.
My heart was opened to receive every form:
It is a meadow where gazelles graze,
It is a convent of Christian monks,
It is a temple of idols,
It is the Kaaba of the pilgrims,
It is the tablets of the Thora,
It is the book of the Koran.
I follow the religion of love:
No matter which path
the camels of love are taking,
There is my confession,
There is my faith."

Dedication

I dedicate this book to my father Albert Hellinger (1895–1967) with a letter:

Dear Dad,

For such a long time I did not know what I was missing deep, deep inside. For such a long time, you, my dear Dad, were banned from my heart. For such a long time you were just someone who was there. I hardly noticed you, as my gaze was focused on something else, on something greater, as I imagined.

Suddenly you returned to me as if from far away, because my wife Sophie called you. She saw you, and you spoke to me through her.

When I think about how often and how much I felt bigger than you, how very much afraid of you I was, because you often beat me very badly and I banned you from my heart, yes I had to, because my mother got in between us, well only now do I feel how empty and lonely I had become and how separated I felt from the full life.

But now you have returned into my life from very far away, lovingly and with some distance, without interfering in my life. Only now do I begin to grasp that it was you who secured our survival day after day, without our feeling deep down how much love was flowing from you to us, always the same, always focused on our well-being, and yet as if excluded from our hearts. Have we ever told you how great you were as our father?

You had a sense of loneliness around you, and yet you stayed with us. You remained conscientious and loving in the service of our life and our future. We took it for granted, without ever acknowledging what it demanded of you.

Now tears come to my eyes, dear Dad. I bow to your greatness and I take you into my heart. You were as if excluded from my heart for such a long time. It was so empty without you.

And even now you remain at some distance from me in a friendly way, without expecting anything that could take away from your greatness and your dignity. As my father you remain the big one, and I take you and everything I owe to you, as your beloved son.

Dear Dad,
Your Toni

(This is what I was called in my family as a child)

Appendix

Biography

Anton Hellinger, born in 1925, later on mainly known as Bert Hellinger, joined the Catholic order of the Mariannhill Missionaries at age 20. He studied philosophy and theology at the university of Würzburg, became a priest and then he was sent to the diocese Mariannhill in South Africa. In South Africa he was involved in further studies at the University of Natal and at the university of South Africa, finishing with a University Education Diploma. Then he was given a position in the diocese Mariannhill in pastoral care, and later was made the principal of one of the leading schools for indigenous Africans in South Africa. In South Africa he became acquainted with group dynamics, which he applied with good results in his school.

Sixteen years later he received a call from his order to come back to Germany to lead the seminary of the missionaries of Mariannhill in Würzburg.

Two years later he left the order and the priesthood. He began a psychoanalytic training, which he completed as an officially recognized psychoanalyst. At the same time he began offering seminars in group dynamics, which he broadened step by step with the methods in which he was also comprehensively trained at the time.

Amongst them those that stood out were the transaction analysis and the script analysis of Eric Berne, the hypnotherapy according to Milton H. Erickson, and the Primal Therapy by and with Arthur Janov.

Only in 1979 did he come across family constellations, the method to which his name is now primarily connected. His insights into "the orders of love" – which is also the title of his first book – made family constellations known worldwide, and he has been presenting these in large seminars all over the world ever since.

These insights are of a philosophical nature. Hellinger gained these insights through the application of the philosophical method of phenomenology. The intensive application of this method over the years has resulted in many books written by him about applied wisdom of life, especially recently. The book you are holding in your hands belongs to this series too.

Contacts

Online Shop
www.Hellinger-Shop.com

Homepage
www.Hellinger.com

Email:
info@Hellingerschule.com

Learning with Hellinger
On his website www.Hellinger.com
you'll find the list of all seminars by Hellinger
and the Hellinger School worldwide.

Bert Hellinger
Natural Transcendence
200 pages, 1. Edition 2009
Hellinger Publications
ISBN 978-3-00-029159-3

Defying easy categorization, Natural Transcendence is a daring book: daring to explore the essential territory of our existence, daring to ask the fundamental questions, daring to share insights as they evolve over time. Sure-footed and open, Bert Hellinger presents a confident perspective, equally comfortable in what appears to be known and in what is by definition beyond knowing.

His willingness to navigate this terrain is an irresistible consequence of decades of investigation and assimilation both of the outer world and the inner sphere; in that convergence Bert Hellinger has found access to the overarching, creative force that is at work in all things. Not meant to be a final declarative statement of reason and purpose, but rather a glimpse, this book offers specific and broad imaginings of what it means for ones life to be in tune with this force.

Natural Transcendence may sit on the bedside table, picked up and read before dreaming, or perhaps in the morning before the tasks of the day take over. It is thought-provoking, and more, it is feeling-provoking; it is an invitation to new levels of profound awareness and an invitation to step into the fresh fullness of life.

Bert Hellinger
Living Trancendence
216 pages, large format,
First Edition 2010
Hellinger Publications,
ISBN 978-3-00-029326-9

What is known is vast. What is unknown can only be glimpsed. And while many of us climb sand dunes trying to grasp some small aspect of the first, others of us attempt to negotiate the latter, usually trying to make it manageable by squeezing the unfathomable into the limitations of our understanding. The dilemma is that we are aware that there is more to life, to us, than all human-initiated study can tell, and at the same time, we sense that the mystery is unattainable, so that any attempt to unravel the riddle will inevitably prove futile.

Living Transcendence accounts for what is known and what cannot be known and even for the ephemeral nature of the thoughts communicated within it. It is both rooted and free-flowing in its impressions of what it means to live in the expansiveness of lifes dynamic trajectories without retreating into the illusion of control.

Bert Hellinger has always been a traveler who keeps copious track of the images along the way. His direction is set toward the endlessly unfolding. As readers, we pick up these notes to find a radical philosophy of all-encompassing love that addresses all of our deepest sorrows and most difficult challenges. The answers are not in the details but in the complete shift from narrow to broad, from individual isolation to the assumption of connectedness.

To return to this natural state takes practice, but it first takes someone to remind us that we may have let it slip away. Bert Hellinger does thatvand then he tells us what he has learned about being in accordance with rather than in opposition to this love. This state of empowered surrender is what we will come to know as living transcendence.

Printed in Poland
by Amazon Fulfillment
Poland Sp. z o.o., Wrocław

31192061R00065